PENGUIN BOOKS

Feminist Fight Club

'I'll be buying this for any young woman I know starting out on her career . . . It is invaluable wisdom' *Sunday Times*

'Funny and fresh . . . One of those books that every person, not just every woman, should read' *Glamour*

'Seriously useful . . . *Feminist Fight Club* is a perfect gift for the friend who just needs a little push to start standing up for herself' *Refinery29*

'*Feminist Fight Club* is a worthy addition to the library of any young female professional or frustrated middle manager or male co-worker who wants to help' *Fortune*

'*Lean In* conceived as an illustrated guide for millennials. *Feminist Fight Club* is as grounded in academic research as *Lean In* . . . Ms Bennett manages to convey a remarkable amount of substance briskly and entertainingly . . . it has performed a huge service not just to its target audience but to the businesses they will be joining' *The New York Times*

'*Feminist Fight Club* is engaging, hilarious and practical – full of simple tools for battling workplace sexism that every woman should have at her disposal. Jessica is a unique voice – and I will proudly proclaim myself a card-carrying member of the FFC' Sheryl Sandberg, COO of Facebook and bestselling author of *Lean In*

'A classic, f*ck-you feminist battle guide, with unapologetic strategies for how to get down and strength up with female comrades to fight patriarchy on the daily. Every woman should have a Feminist Fight Club' Ilana Glazer, comedian and co-creator of *Broad City*

'This book offers the weapons that women need to win the war on inequality. With mighty wit, Jessica Bennett shows women how to defeat the enemies – a_____. I was not prepared_____ so much about a s_____ *Originals*

FFC FOREVER

* This book is 21 percent more expensive for men

FEMINIST FIGHT CLUB

A SURVIVAL MANUAL

(for a SEXIST WORKPLACE)

JESSICA BENNETT

Illustrations by Saskia Wariner
with Hilary Fitzgerald Campbell

PENGUIN BOOKS

PENGUIN BOOKS

UK | USA | Canada | Ireland | Australia
India | New Zealand | South Africa

Penguin Books is part of the Penguin
Random House group of companies
whose addresses can be found at global.penguinrandomhouse.com.

 Penguin
Random House
UK

First published in the United States of America by Harper Wave,
an imprint of HarperCollins Publishers 2016
First published in Great Britain by Portfolio 2016
Published in Penguin Books 2017
001

Illustrations by Saskia Wariner with Hilary Fitzgerald Campbell

Background graphic on page 88 by Miloje/Shutterstock, Inc.
Ink splatters throughout by AnaWhite/Shutterstock, Inc.
Grenade illustration by Kovalenko Alexander/Shutterstock, Inc.
Fist art by Zmiter/Shutterstock, Inc.

Printed in Great Britain by Clays Ltd, St Ives plc

A CIP catalogue record for this book is
available from the British Library

ISBN: 978-0-241-24484-5

TO MY OWN FEMINIST FIGHT CLUB:

the ultimate squad, sisterhood, girl army, #pussyposse, and battle comrades a gal could ask for.

You are my queens.

Contents

HOW TO READ THIS BOOK

PATRIARCHY

FEMINISM

There is no right way to read this book. Read it front to back, open it in the middle, or treat it like a cookbook*: flip to the sections you like best, write in the margins, take notes in the back, tear out pages, or slide them underneath your boss's door.

The goal of this book is to provide you with battle tactics: simple, easy to follow, effective tricks for combatting sexist, subtly sexist, overtly sexist, and sometimes just *oblivious* behaviors that exist in even our most progressive offices.

Much of what you'll read here is inspired by my own experiences, as well as those of colleagues, sources, and friends. But it is also

---

* A thing, to my mother's dismay, I have never owned.

backed up by *data*: vetted, published, peer-reviewed research you can find documented at the end. The tone of this book may be light, but its basis is not—and not a premise or a fight move exists without statistical evidence to back it up.

This book won't describe every character nor every workplace. But my hope is that there is something in it for everyone, no matter their career level or economic class, their race, sexual orientation, or gender identity. I am writing for women, but I am also writing for men—because you, male feminists, are crucial to this battle.

Feminist Fight Club is a manual, it is a manifesto, but it's also a choose-your-own-adventure—left in the hands of you, the reader, to carry forward. I hope you will.

FEMINIST FIGHT CLUB

STARTER KIT

THIS IDEA BELONGS TO

1   FOR SHUTTING UP MANTERRUPTERS

2   MAKE YOUR VOICE HEARD!

3   TO DRY MALE TEARS

4   FOR KEEPING HAIR OUT OF EYES DURING BATTLE

5   PREVENT BROPROPRIATION WITH THIS HANDY STAMP

6   BECAUSE: WHISKEYYYYYY

fem-i-nist / n.
A person who believes in equality between
men and women. (YOU!)

pa-tri-ar-chy / n.
A system that was created by and for men, in
everything from language (human) to your
office temperature (yes, that AC is actually
set to a temp most comfortable to the XY
chromosome).
   No, not every man is part of the patriarchy.
But we do refer to the patriarchy as The Man.

Fem-i-nist Fight Club / n.
Your crew, your posse, your girl gang; your
unconditionally helpful professional support
system; your ride-or-die homies. Down with
the patriarchy!

RULES OF THE FEMINIST FIGHT CLUB

Rule No.1 : You must talk about the Feminist Fight Club

Rule No.2 : You **MUST** talk about the Feminist Fight Club !!!

Rule No.3 : We fight PATRIARCHY, not each other

Rule No.4 : Membership to the FFC means you've taken an oath to help other women — **all** women. Vagffirm your fellow fighters.

Rule No.5 : The FFC is inclusive and non-hierarchical. Everyone's an equal fighter.

Rule No.6 : If someone yells stop, goes limp, taps out, the fight is still not over. The fight is not over until we have achieved equality for ALL women.

Rule No.7 : Whi-i-i-i-ich might be a while. So put on your favorite sweats.

Rule No.8 : No wallflowers. Everyone must fight !

Introduction:

PREPARE FOR BATTLE

"The law cannot do it for us. We must do it for ourselves. Women in this country must become revolutionaries."

—Shirley Chisholm, the first African American woman elected to the U.S. Congress

It was a fight club—except without the fighting and without the men. Every month or so, a dozen of us—women in our twenties and thirties, struggling writers and creative types, most of us with second jobs—would gather at a friend's apartment (actually, her parents' apartment: none of us had an apartment big enough to fit that many people). She'd provide the pasta, salad, or pasta salad, and we'd bring the wine (and seltzer . . . for some reason we all really liked seltzer). We'd pile our plates high and sink into the cushioned couches in her living room to talk—or, bitch, rather—about our jobs.

In those early days, the rules of the fight club were simple:

> What was said in the group stayed in the group.
> Members were never to speak the group's name.
> And we practiced strict vag-cronyism.

That is, membership was not based on merit but *vagina*. Which meant that once you were in, you were in: engulfed in bosom-like support, embraced and respected, encouraged with finger snaps and fist bumps and cat videos, but no cattiness. We had a strict no "mean girls" policy.

The fact that the club was kept a secret basically justified its need. We were smart, ambitious women striving to "make it" in New York, a city that eats the soft alive. We had grown up in an era of Girl Power—Spice Girls, you know it—when it wasn't simply an encouragement but an *expectation* that girls could be and do whatever they wanted. And we believed it. The gender war, we thought, was a relic of our mother's generation—a battle won long ago.

And yet each of us, in every field, in every role, was stumbling into gender land mines at seemingly every turn—and often ones we didn't even know existed. It was like trying to dodge that stench that lurks on a New York City street on a hot summer night: there you were, minding your own business, and *BAM*.

Our meetings had a moderator, of sorts—our host. Sometimes she'd hand out note cards containing handwritten questions. *(Where do you want to be in five years? What's one way you plan to help another woman this year? Who's your favorite female perfor— Oh wait, duh, Beyoncé.)* There were times we'd gather in smaller, informal settings as needed: if one of us had a crisis, an upcoming job interview, an article due, an impending mental breakdown, or looming unemployment—which nearly every one of us had faced at one point or another.

But usually we simply hung out, ate snacks, shot the shit, and talked about work.

I've vowed to keep their details secret, but the group looked something like this: Danielle, a brilliantly funny writer, had been toiling away as an assistant at a well-known TV show (a show that, at that time, had not a single female writer). On the side, she'd written two books, created web videos, and taught herself Photoshop—mostly so she could make colorful invitations to Fight Club meetings. But at work, she was consistently passed over for promotions. Tired, disgruntled, and dying of boredom, she had taken to mining the web for inspirational lady-news to send to get us through the day. That, and making feminist cat sweatshirts. Did any of us know somewhere she could try to sell them?

Nola, a project manager at an ad agency, had recently emailed us all in a rage. She was leading a top-level client meeting when one of her male colleagues had asked if she wouldn't mind grabbing some coffee for the group. Stunned, she found herself trudging to the kitchen to complete the task. She returned to the meeting with a coffee stain down the front of her blouse and daggers shooting from her eyes.

There was another woman, a straight-shooting web developer named Rachel, whose male boss told her she was "too aggressive" with her staff. Everyone knew what that was code for: too loud, a little bossy, not "ladylike" enough, according to some made-up standard. But this woman was good at her job—that was never in question. So why should *the volume of her voice* have mattered?

There was a documentary filmmaker, Tanya, who told a story of having her idea for a show handed off to a male colleague to produce. She was livid. But she stayed quiet, not wanting to be viewed as too "emotional" (or a poor team player). If any of us got wind of any production openings, please, *please* send them her way.

I was working at Tumblr at the time, my job part of a widely touted initiative to hire journalists to create content on a blogging platform most commonly known for GIFs (and porn). The perks of a tech company were shiny, for a second: Free meals. Endless snacks. Bring your dog to work day . . . every day. Fancy cold-brew coffee, and the hot "brewmaster" named Grady who would deliver it. Unlimited vacation. A kegerator that would ID you (and your beer preferences) by your fingerprint. A ping-pong table for when you got back from your vacation, finished your personalized beer, played with your dog and just wanted to . . . you know, *relax, man.*

And then there were the annoyingly bro-y things: said ping-pong table was six feet from my desk. (No, really—ping-pong balls ricocheting off my laptop were a daily occurrence.) Off-site field trips consisted of basketball games and Medieval Times, and in-office social hour meant a brotastic round of all-staff flip cup—again, on the ping-pong table, feet from my desk.

ME AT TUMBLR

But at the core of the problem was the job itself. I'd been hired along with another editor, whom I'd met and liked. We would be co-editors, I was told, and would both report to the CEO. Which was sort of true except that I had accepted the job before we had finalized my title. (Note to self: *never* accept a job without formalizing the title, even if you're told you'll get to "choose" your own.) I was informed casually that'd he'd chosen the title of editor in chief. As in: the highest possible title a person in our field could hold, typically reserved for the absolute ruler of an editorial outfit. But, no worries, the HR manager assured me, we were all part of a *suuuuper* flat structure here—so what title did I want? (I chose "executive editor.")

Now in reality, it was not all bad: said colleague, the editor in chief, was a great guy. (A feminist, even!) Married to a power lawyer, the father of two adorable kids. Progressive! Supportive! Jovial! And yet the fact remained: I had been sneak-attacked with a surprise boss, and that boss was a dude.

I could have complained, had the hiring director—or "head of people," as he was called—not been fired days after I arrived. (Why would a hundred-person company need an HR department?) Still, my boss was an experienced manager. He knew how to command respect in an all-male room. He spoke sternly and authoritatively, whereas I got nervous. People looked at him, not me, in the meetings anyway— he *looked like* a boss—whether we were talking about a project he was running or not. He would try to help—repeating my ideas with the vocal authority of a six-foot-two, forty-two-year-old white man who was trying to be my advocate. But then he'd get credit for them, too.

I was there too short a time for any of this to really matter: we were all laid off abruptly just over a year after we started, the precursor to an acquisition by a larger company (Yahoo).

But truth was, this was hardly the first time I'd found myself in such a scenario.

I had begun my career at one of the oldest of the old boys' clubs, *Newsweek,* where the sexism had once been so rife that the female staffers—led by a young civil rights lawyer, now congresswoman, named Eleanor Holmes Norton—sued the company for gender discrimination in what was the first lawsuit of its kind. It was 1970, and the *Newsweek* women were brimming with privilege and smarts: Fulbright scholars, valedictorians, graduates of Seven Sisters colleges from well-off families. As Norton would describe it later: "These were women who you would think wouldn't have anything to fear at work."

And yet they were told bluntly that "women don't write." They were called "dollies" by their male bosses. Their job duties included pushing mail carts and delivering coffee as well as real research and reporting, all three requiring handing something over to a man. "It was a very hopeless time," said Susan Brownmiller, a feminist scholar who—along with the late director and screenwriter Nora Ephron—was a *Newsweek* researcher (i.e., "mail girl") for a brief period in the 1960s. Both decamped before the lawsuit, but the words of a researcher who remained always stuck in my mind: "After a while you really did start to lose your confidence," she told me. "You started to think, 'Writing is what the men do.'"

```
Nora Ephron's first job was as a Newsweek "mail
girl" in 1962. In her interview, she was asked
why she wanted the job.
    "I want to be a writer," she said.
    "Women don't write at Newsweek," she was told.
```

I never knew that story, in part because the legacy had not been passed down. And yet four decades later, during my era, the experience felt familiar: writing was what "the men" did. I *was* a writer, of course. I held the title to prove it—as did many of my female colleagues. But our work was still published with a fraction of the frequency of the male staffers at that time. We had not been promoted as quickly as the male colleagues we'd arrived with. And it was hard not to notice that the leaders of the struggling newsweekly were almost entirely white and male. Later, we would add up the bylines for that calendar year: men would write all but six of the magazine's forty-nine cover stories.

Still, *Newsweek* was a cushy job for a young journalist. It was my first real job out of college, and I felt lucky* to have landed it. But it was also the first time that I began to doubt my skill. I wasn't very good at talking myself up, and I stumbled when asked to pitch my ideas to a room—typically to a roomful of men. I didn't know how to react when

---

* Luck: a thing that women give credit to for their success. What men give credit to: skill.

a basketball hoop was erected in the newsroom, or when the new boss began spending all his time hanging out by my desk. I didn't have a mentor I could talk to. In fact, there were few senior women to speak of.

It wasn't *blatant* sexism . . . exactly. There could never be a formal policy that banned women from writing; to the contrary, the door was open to women, and we were rolling through it in greater numbers than ever. But those long-ingrained attitudes don't just evaporate in a generation.

ANY NEWS GUY

white

male

sparkly shoes

The *New York Times* columnist Gail Collins once told me that while the sexism of her era was certainly crushing, it also had a kind of benefit: it was easy to identify. When a guy pinched your ass or told you that "women don't write at *Newsweek*" it certainly wasn't fair, but at least you *knew* it wasn't fair. It was clear-cut discrimination—sexism with a legal definition and a thumbprint—not simply a "feeling." *(Was it real? Am I crazy? Was I the only one who saw it?)*

Recognizing sexism is harder than it once was. Like the micro-aggressions that people of color endure daily—racism masked as subtle insults or dismissals—today's sexism is insidious, casual, politically correct, even *friendly*. It is a kind of can't-put-your-finger-on, not-particularly-overt, hard-to-quantify, harder-even-to-call-out behavior that maybe isn't necessarily intentional, or conscious. Sometimes women exhibit it too. None of that makes it any less damaging.

On a day-to-day level, it's watching a man instinctively turn to a woman to take notes in a meeting, or being mistaken for the admin when you're actually the one in charge. It's being talked over in a group setting, over and over again,* or having your idea attributed to someone else (more often than not a dude). It's following all the rules, leaning all the way in, and *still* having to worry about being perceived as "too aggressive" when you display the behavior required of a person in charge. It's knowing that a colleague calling another woman "ambitious" is the opposite of a compliment. It's having to be nice (because women are nice!) but not *too* nice (don't wanna be a pushover); maternal (a natural caretaker!), but not *actually* a mother (lest you be viewed as "uncommitted" to the job). It's having to be confident so that you can command respect but not *too* confident (because we don't like cocky women). It's having to work twice as hard to prove you're once as good, or three, four, five times as hard if you happen to be female *and* of color.

> **sub-tle sex-ism / n.**
> The kind of sexism that makes you wonder, *Am I actually just crazy?* (No, you are not.)

It is the fact that women are still more likely than men to feel like imposters, or that when men rise up through the ranks, we like them more, but when women rise, we like them less (which is why women have to make sure to smile frequently, show gratitude and concern, emphasize communal goals, be appreciative . . . you get the drill).

---

* Yes, women are interrupted in meetings (by both men and women) at twice the rate of men.

Some call this form of sexism Death by a Thousand Cuts. Taken individually, the affronts don't seem like that big a deal. But over time, and collectively, they are fatal.

If you take the longitudinal view, there are a lot of positives about the state of gender equality today. Women are graduating from college in higher numbers, earning more graduate degrees and PhDs, dominating social media, engaging in online activism, and—for perhaps the first time ever—seeing themselves reflected back in television and pop culture. (All hail Shonda Rhimes!) Women hold the vast majority of consumer spending power in this country and, by 2018, wives will outearn husbands.

And yet.

In their first year out of college, even *after* accounting for all the things that could affect one's wages—job choice, job type, hours worked, taking time off, and so forth—women still (*still!*) earn just 93 percent what their male peers do. Women of all races and ethnicities will be one-quarter as likely to negotiate a raise—and will be deemed pushy or aggressive when they try to. Some of these are privileged problems, no doubt, but these same problems can be viewed as even more acute for the 42 million women in America on the brink of poverty.

The stats show clearly that there is a social benefit to changing the paradigm. Businesses are more successful when they hire women: more collaborative, more profitable, more inclusive.* Women are in fact more effective leaders, less likely to take unnecessary risks, great at multitasking, and have higher emotional intelligence—as the *Harvard Business Review* put it, "one of the least counter-intuitive findings in the social sciences." True gender equality, research has shown, would increase the U.S. GDP by 26 percent.

In an ideal scenario, we'd have policies in place to ensure that our workplaces are equal—and hopefully we'll get there. But even if some scholars believe that it's the female leadership style that will fuel the revolution (and they do), even if we are working on a political level toward *systemic* change (wage equality and paid family leave, for instance), even if *every pop star in the world* proclaims herself a feminist (thank you, Bey!), most of us still have to roll out of bed each morning feeling relatively powerless and face the mundane, boring, subtle bullshit that confronts us on a daily basis. Diversity trainings don't solve for being the default "coffee girl;" our legal system isn't equipped

---

* Fun fact: When Google cofounders Larry Page and Sergey Brin decided to bring on Marissa Mayer, the company's first female engineer, they told her, "We've read a lot of books, and we know that organizations work better when there is gender balance."

to solve for the fact that strong women will be perceived as "pushy" or the fact that Americans still prefer male bosses. Just look at Ellen Pao.

And so.

We need weapons of our own, then—an *arsenal* of them. We must be armed with data to prove the problem exists and tactics to chip away at it from the outside *and* the inside. We need skills, hacks, tricks, tools, battle tactics to fight for ourselves while *also* advocating for change within the system.

But!

This is not a solo task.

We need other women by our side.

So let's start by linking arms.

When my Fight Club began, the first rule was simple: we did not talk about the club. Anonymity was crucial: this wasn't a networking group or a place to rack up LinkedIn connections. It was where we could vent and cry and scream and laugh—all without the fear of judgment (or blind items ending up on *Gawker*).

For years, the Fight Club tactics were passed quietly between us, cradled like precious gems. But the time has come to talk about the club—and not just quietly in somebody's living room.

This book is for women who, like us, have observed sexist behavior but convinced themselves it wasn't really a problem (or that the problem was their fault). It is for the woman who knows she belongs at the table but doesn't have the confidence—or tools—to feel like she can take a seat (or know what to do once she's there). It's about knowing that the challenges are collective and to empower you—yes, you!—to become too wily, too informed, too prepared for anyone, or any system, to limit you. Within every woman exists a warrior. Really.

There is an old-school anthology from the 1970s that I kept on my desk while I wrote this book—a yellowed text with a red raised fist on its cover that lit a match to the modern women's movement. The book is called *Sisterhood Is Powerful,* and it begins with a simple phrase: "This book is an action."

This book, too, is an action. It is an action, an attitude, a state of mind, a collective call to arms.

Welcome to the Feminist Fight Club.
This is not a drill.

The FFC

WOMANIFESTO

WHAT IS THE FFC?

The FFC is an alliance among women ages zero to infinity with the goal of world domination. It represents all women who are kicking ass and taking names, those who would like to, and the men who support them. It is women who are finished with the sexist status quo and those who haven't yet realized they are angry. Welcome to the club. You have lifelong membership.

WHAT DOES THE FFC HOPE TO ACCOMPLISH?

More female heads of state; more women—and not just white women—who are scientists, engineers, late-night talk show hosts, showrunners. We want to make it rain Tubmans (the new face of the $20 bill) but we also want a woman on the hundred-dollar bill—and the fifty, the ten, and the five. We want to eradicate sexist language and being told to "smile!" We strive for equal wages, government-subsidized paid family leave, and maybe even company-covered egg freezing for all. Our approach is three-pronged: fight for ourselves, fight for our sisters, fight the system.

HOW CAN I IDENTIFY A MEMBER OF THE FFC?

Mwahaha, good luck—we have mastered the art of blending in. Members of the FFC may look like "regular" women, and we could be anywhere: tweeting about *Veep;* bringing orange slices to your kid's soccer game; swiping left on your Tinder; running your company or running next to you at the gym. Despite this tricky camouflage, be warned: FFC members are rigorously trained in statistical warfare, negotiation, and blocking micro-aggressions as well as grueling physical combat. We know computer code, how to dismantle a grenade *and* Missy Elliott lyrics.

ARE THERE WAYS I CAN MAKE MY WORKPLACE MORE FRIENDLY TO MEMBERS OF THE FFC?

You can start with a lactation room that doesn't double as a broom closet. Other possible enticements: an office temperature above fifty-five degrees; copies of *Nice Girls Don't Get the Corner Office* casually placed on the desks of male bosses. Hosting karaoke nights instead of beer pong isn't a bad idea (we have to practice our battle hymns somewhere). Oh, and stop yourself the next time you have the urge to ask your eight-months pregnant coworker if she's "looking forward to her time off."

CAN MEN ENLIST IN THE FFC?

Yes! And we encourage them to do so. The easiest way to enlist in the Men's Auxiliary is to flip immediately to page 239 for a very special

PSA: that is—a Penile Service Announcement. Now print it out, stuff it inside your *Bossypants*, and set up shop at your local coffeehouse until someone recruits you. *Just be cool*. We'll know you when we see you (and we'll take a cappuccino, thanks). Other recruitment depots include the spiraling line outside the women's bathroom; the "feminism" section of your local indie bookstore; lesbian dive bars; poetry slams; Hillary Clinton canvassing centers.

Somebody will be in touch.

* A tip of the Brontë bonnet to humorist Shannon Reed, whose "Spinster Agenda" for the *New Yorker*'s Daily Shouts inspired this manifesto.

Part One

KNOW THE ENEMY

BEHAVIOR to
WATCH
OUT for

Let's go back to the beginning.

The Feminist Fight Club was founded in 2009—but we made no claim of being the first group of women to meet in a cramped apartment to complain about our jobs. In my mother's era, the weekly gatherings were called consciousness-raising groups: women who would meet, often while somebody's husband was away, to ask one another, *How do you feel about housework? What do you want to do in life? Have you ever faked an orgasm?*

The groups would become the backbone of the women's movement: publishing underground newspapers, lobbying for policy, and staging many a protest. There was a sit-in at the *Ladies' Home Journal,* to demand a female editor; an ogle-in on Wall Street, where women cat-called men; and a famous demonstration at the 1968 Miss America Pageant, where protesters tossed their bras, girdles, and high heels into a "Freedom Trash Can."* Each of the groups had different tactics, and they disagreed on much, but what they shared was the belief that, as the organizer Kathie Sarachild put it, women were "about the most exciting people around." Sarachild had been part of a group called New York Radical Women. (She also coined the phrase "Sisterhood is Powerful.")

---

* Feminist fun-fact: This is where the term "bra burning" originated—though it never actually happened. The Miss America protesters had indeed *planned* to burn bras, but they couldn't get the right permit—but the *New York Post* ran with the headline anyway and the image stuck.

My own Feminist Fight Club was forged one afternoon on the upper level of a Manhattan McDonald's, over milkshakes and fries. It was just three women then, each low-level staffers working in television, not long after Barack Obama had secured the presidency, and Congress had made not a single gain in female representation (for the first time since 1978). It also happened to be the year that David Letterman would admit to sleeping with his assistant; that an ESPN analyst would be fired for having a relationship with a young staffer; and Chris Brown would be charged with assaulting his then-girlfriend, Rihanna.

Those scandals were the backdrop, but the catalyst was personal. One of the women, a research assistant, had been performing the duties of a job two rungs above her pay grade for more than a year—but without the title or compensation. (When she asked to be promoted, she was told it "wasn't the right time.") Another, after four years as an assistant, had indeed been "promoted," but without a raise or a direct boss. She was now sitting in a windowless closet she called the "cloffice" (closet-office), next to the mail room, where the top boss stored his dry cleaning. She hung up one of those peel-and-stick wall decals—a Caribbean beach scene—to stave off her claustrophobia.

"We felt like we were stuck, and we had no means of getting out," she explained later. "We had no network, no mentors. And I think we recognized early that—in our office anyway—a man's opinion just meant more."

The first formal meeting took place on a Friday night, at the apartment of the cloffice-dweller's parents, who'd been banished to the bedroom (we tiptoed through to use the bathroom). There were a dozen women there that night, and we voted on a name. (Among the rejected titles: V.A.G.I.N.A., or Very Angry Girls in New York Media Associations, docked for its narrowness—both the vagina and the media—and the Cat Pack, vetoed for its cat-lady connotation.) We were to bring something to read aloud, either written by a woman, about a woman, or inspiring to women. There would be dinner, but we would not be eating "like *girls*." We were told to come hungry.

Most there that night had never met: we were a hodgepodge of friends of friends, acquaintances, and colleagues twice removed. (I'd been introduced through a mentor who was friends with our host's mother.) But we were all about the same age, in creative-ish fields, at roughly the same point in our careers. We had certain New York neuroses that bound us. Each of us was privileged: we were college graduates with decent apartments, if not big enough to fit the group. We had second and third jobs, but the reason was so we could pursue what we really wanted to do.

"We will not be eating 'like girls,'" the invite noted, "so please come hungry."

Nevertheless, there was a sense that somehow, before this moment—as we sat in a semicircle, shoving cheese into our mouths—we were alone. Most of us had never talked openly about these issues. Many of us had questioned if we were part of the problem. We weren't completely naive: we knew sexism existed. But this was a different form of it—subtler, friendlier, more insidious.

How, one woman wanted to know, could she get the guy who always interrupted her in meetings to *shut up* without seeming defensive or overly sensitive? What could she do, another asked, when her ideas were presented by a male colleague without proper credit? None of this was overt discrimination. Often, these actions were perpetrated by guys we *liked*. But that was part of the problem. After thousands of years of being treated as the dominant sex—and learning to act with the authority, speech, and body language that come along with that status—these are the behaviors that even the nice guys had picked up. How could we work together to call them out?

It wasn't rocket science—we realized this. But at the time, it did feel like a kind of awakening. That moment of validation when you realize that the problem isn't just *you*.* And if it wasn't just us, then suddenly we could chip away at it—because we had other women to back us up.

We didn't state it out loud, but I think each of us made a decision that night that we were going to take this on. That, together, we felt strong enough to combat this strangely subtle enemy. That the fight

---

* Or what second-wave feminists called the "click"

might even be fun. We might not win—but you'd better believe we would go down swinging.

After
thousands of years
of being treated as the
dominant sex—and learning to
act with the authority, speech,
and body language that come
along with that status—these
are the behaviors that even
the nice guys had
picked up.

The Enemy:
THE MANTERRUPTER

A quick pop culture history refresher: remember that moment back in 2009, when Kanye West lunged onto the stage at the VMAs, grabbed the microphone out of Taylor Swift's hand, and launched into a monologue? "Imma let you finish," he said, as Swift stood by in stunned silence. "But Beyoncé had one of the best videos of all time!"

Whether or not you agreed with his musical assessment (or the fact that he had appointed himself spokesman for another powerful woman) it was the most publicly memorable instance of a manterruption—a man interrupting a woman while she was trying to speak (in this case, on a stage, *alone*, trying to accept the award for best female video). But to a certain breed of working woman, Kanye's behavior was familiar. We speak up in a meeting, only to hear a man's voice boom over ours. We chime in with an idea, perhaps a tad too uncertainly—and a dude interjects with authority. We may have the ideas, but he has the vocal cords—causing us to clam up, lose our confidence, or cede credit for our work. Studies show the Manterrupter is real: men speak more than women in professional meetings, they interrupt more frequently, and women are *twice* as likely as men to be interrupted by both men and women when they speak (and even more if they're a woman of color). It's not just Taylor who gets shafted.

THE FIGHT MOVES

Verbal Chicken

This is the verbal equivalent of two cars racing toward each other attop speed until one (his) swerves. Your job is to stay strong and *just keep talking*. Keep your pauses short. Maintain your momentum. No matter if he waves his hands, raises his voice, or squirms in his chair, *do you*. Pretend to be deaf if you have to; it's worth it if it helps you make your point. The key is to prevent him from getting a word in while simultaneously acting like you are the chillest person in the room. That, and a side-eye that says, "DON'T YOU DARE FUCKING INTERRUPT ME."

Womanterruption

Sure, you can call out a Manterrupter: "Bob, I wasn't done finishing that point. Give me one more sec." But imagine for a second if Beyoncé had walked up onstage where Kanye was busy interrupting Taylor and interrupted *him*. This is what we call womanterruption, or interrupting a Manterrupter on behalf of your fellow woman. If you hear an idea from another woman that you think is good, back her up: "Wait, can you let her finish?" If you can tell a woman can't get a word in, interject and ask a question: "Nell, what is your opinion?" You'll have more of an effect than you might think—*and* you'll establish yourself as a team player.

Lean In (Literally)

In one study, researchers found that men physically lean in more than women during seated meetings, making them less likely to be interrupted. (Lyndon B. Johnson was famous for his lean.) Other methods of asserting your physical space when you have something important to say: Sitting at the table instead of in the back of the room, pointing to someone, standing up, placing your hand on the table, or making eye contact. Bonus tip: men often arrive at meetings early in order to get a good seat. It's not a bad idea in general to place yourself in the *closest physical proximity* to where the important conversations are being held or decisions are being made.

Kanye-Free Zone

If you're in a position of power: establish a no Kanye-ing rule. People *do not* interrupt—as policy—while people are speaking or pitching, and those who try to grab the mic will be shamed. If you must, employ that elementary school tool of the talking stick. You may laugh, but the manager of a seven-hundred-person team at Google says she employs this method.

MANTERRUPTING CONTRACT

I, _____, will
try my best __not__ to interrupt my
colleagues.

Instead I will :

_____

_____

_____

_____

_____

_____

Shh...

_____   _____
Interruptor Signature   Date

The Enemy:
THE BROPROPRIATOR

You could argue that our country was founded on a bropropriation of sorts: a white man (Columbus) and his crew (more white dudes) claiming credit for discovering a New World that wasn't actually new (or theirs). In an office setting, the Bropropriator appropriates credit for another's work: presenting the ideas of his team as his own, accepting credit for an idea that wasn't his, or sometimes even doing nothing at all and *still* ending up with credit—a convenient reality of being born male, where credit is *assumed*.* When it comes to women in particular, bropropriation is backed up by fact: women are less likely to have their ideas correctly attributed to them, and we have a centuries-long history to prove it.

---

* Yeah, so, in a situation where men and women work together on a project, research has found that colleagues (or bosses) tend to infer that it is the men who deserve the credit. Argh!

THE FIGHT MOVES

👊 Tough Talk

It's pretty hard for someone to take credit for your idea if you deliver it with such authority that nobody can forget it. So speak up—no *ums*, *sorrys*, or baby voice allowed. Use active, authoritative words that show you're taking ownership of what you're saying. Not "I wonder what would happen if we tried . . ." but "I'd suggest we try . . ."

👊 Thank 'n' Yank

Yank the credit right back—by thanking them for liking your idea. It's a sneaky yet highly effective self-crediting maneuver that still leaves you looking good. Try any version of: "Thanks for picking up on my idea." "Yes! That's exactly the point I was making." "Exactly. So glad you agree—now let's talk about next steps." Sure, sometimes a biting "Is there an echo in here?" may also work, but the thank-n-yank softens the edge.

👊 Wingman

Find a buddy—and maybe even a buddy *who is a dude*. Ask him to nod and look interested when you speak. Let him back you up publicly in meetings. Have him affirm what you say. When somebody tries to take credit for your (or others') work, watch as he speaks up: "Yeah, like Jess said." He corrects the problem, gets applauded for it, and you don't have to say a word.

👊 E-vidence

Keep an email evidence dossier. If you've put forth an incredible idea in public, follow up with an email to your higher-ups summarizing your idea after the meeting—and cc whomever necessary to let them know it's *on the record.*

👊 Snaps

If you hear an idea you like from a woman, support her publicly. Nod; say "yes!"; clap your hands; or even snap your fingers. It's the IRL equivalent of a Facebook "like."

FAMOUS BROPROPRIATIONS

MONOPOLY

Created by an unemployed man named Charles Darrow in the 1930s. Just kidding! It was actually an anti-monopolist, Elizabeth Magie, who dreamed up the game, though Darrow sold it as his own.

COMPUTER CODE

Ada Lovelace wrote the first line of code in 1843—but until recently received no recognition, while her male collaborator got credit.

DNA

Rosalind Franklin's work was crucial to understanding DNA—as well as to the work that would earn her male colleagues the Nobel Prize.

NUCLEAR FISSION

When Lise Meitner's male research partner published the paper they co-wrote, he conveniently omitted her name—and it was he who subsequently won the prize in chemistry from the Royal Swedish Academy of Sciences.

The Enemy:
THE STENOGRAPHUCKER

SEXIST ☑
LAZY ☑
RUDE ☑
INTELLECTUALLY INSULTING ☑
I ADDED ARSENIC ☑

The Stenographucker treats you like the office secretary, even when it's clear you're not: asking casually if you'd "mind taking notes," ccing you on his travel arrangements, or ordering you to "grab coffee" for a client (*your* client). Sometimes he inadvertently assumes you *are* the secretary (or the kitchen help, in the case of Mellody Hobson, the black female chair of the board at DreamWorks).* My friend Alia, who works at a nonprofit, recently attended a cocktail reception for a prestigious scholarship she'd won. Along with the other honoree, a man, she was asked to greet guests at the door. But instead of outstretched hands to congratulate her––those went to the man by her side––she received more than a few coats in her face. People assumed she was the coat-check girl.

---

* In her TED talk, Hobson describes showing up for lunch at a major New York media company—with then-aspiring senator Harold Ford—and the two of them being asked by the receptionist, "Where are your uniforms?"

THE FIGHT MOVES

👊 Bad Barista

Do what digital strategist Aminatou Sow does: when male colleagues ask her to make coffee, she tells them politely that she would be *happy* to do so, if *only she knew how*—her mother told her never to learn how to make coffee so she wouldn't end up having to make it. (The copy-machine equivalent: "I've broken the copy machine so many times, I'm not supposed to touch it.") For further inspiration: see Shel Silverstein's "How Not to Have to Dry the Dishes," which every woman might consider having tattooed to her arm ("If you have to dry the dishes / And you drop one on the floor— / Maybe they won't let you / Dry the dishes anymore.")

👊 Cash In Your Woman Card

Katharine O'Brien, an organizational psychologist, says she uses the following strategy to avoid being disproportionally asked to help out: she says no, and then explains bluntly that she doesn't take meeting notes because she believes it puts women in a subordinate position—of having to *record*, not *speak*. "I've done this for years and I've found it to be very effective," she says. "Most people understand my reasoning and any contention it causes has been fleeting."

👊 Throw to a Bro

That is, backhand* this assignment by suggesting another guy for the job. "I'm actually on the hook for a big presentation right now. But you know who's actually *great* at making spreadsheets? Brad over here. Brad is *excellent* at making spreadsheets." Other possible comebacks include "Would you like me to get you coffee while I'm at it?" and "Are your hands broken?"

👊 Put the Phucker in His Place

I once heard a story of a female CEO who was chastised by a colleague for being out of Diet Coke in a board meeting that *she* was chairing. Instead of getting upset, she turned to the man and said sweetly, "I'll be sure to add that to the agenda for next time." He shut up.

👊 No Volunteers Allowed

Research shows unequivocally that the majority of secretarial tasks fall to women, but women are also more likely to say yes to doing them—and to volunteer of their own accord. We know, saying no can be difficult. But here's one thing that's not: not offering in the first place.

---

* A tennis move that was created by a woman: Bertha Townsend, in 1886.

SHATTERING the CAFFEINE PATRIARCHY

1900

Oklahoma man files for divorce because his wife's coffee isn't up to snuff

1935

"Learn to make good coffee" is offered as advice for "how to stay married" in the New York Times

1973

Alice Johnson, a Naval Air Station Secretary, sues after being fired for her "refusal to make coffee for the guys"

1927

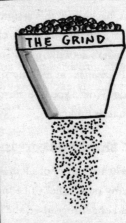

THE GRIND

A man leaves his daughter $50 of his $10K estate because she "once refused to make him coffee"

TODAY

MAKE YOUR OWN DAMN COFFEE

✳ HAT TIP TO "SWIMMING IN THE STENO POOL" BY LYNN PERIL FOR THE AMAZING FACTOIDS

The Enemy:
THE MANSPLAINER

The Mansplainer is smarter than you; ergo, let him just break it down for you real quick. His delivery is typically patronizing or condescending, often inaccurate, and completely lacks nuance—but it comes at you, without variation, as gospel. It's safe to assume that men have been valiantly explaining things to women since—well, since John Adams, who apparently mansplained to Abigail. But until 2008 there was no easy way to describe this concept.

For that we have the Internet to thank—inspired by the novelist Rebecca Solnit, who described in an essay how a man at a party talked over her to convey that *she should really check out this new book*—a book that, had he let her get a word in, he might have learned *she in fact had written* (and he, in fact, had not read). Solnit's essay about it became a book, *Men Explain Things to Me*—and mansplaining was born. Add it to your FFC reading list.

THE FIGHT MOVES

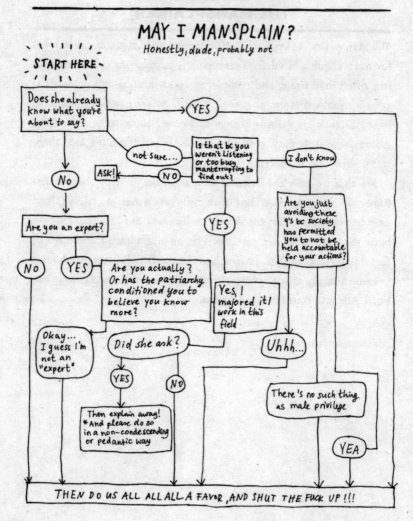

MAY I MANSPLAIN?

Honestly, dude, probably not

The Enemy:
THE HIMITATOR

He's the guy in your creative writing class who restates your interpretation of a poem in an attempt to clarify what you said, but the professor remembers *him* as the one who said it; the dude who puts a great spin on your joke, but then everyone thinks *he* came up with it. He's the colleague who echoes your lesson plan, but then somehow gets seen as the innovator. The Himitator may be less malicious than the Bropropriator in that he is not necessarily stealing your ideas outright—but in the simple act of repeating them, he gets the credit for them anyway.

THE FIGHT MOVES

👊 ReMYnd

Find a way to casually remind the room that the idea began with you. Something like: "Love having your feedback on my [idea/suggestion/proposal]"—the key word being "my." Yes, we ladies like to be team players, but sometimes we need to own the word "mine." If you don't see yourself as deserving ownership of an idea, why will anyone else?

👊 Confront

Don't be afraid to confront your Himitator—maybe he actually thinks he's doing you a favor. If he's your boss, try asking for advice on how you could convey your ideas better on the first round—because you've noticed he tends to restate them. If he's a colleague, tell him you're worried his attempt to *help* you might be backfiring—by you losing credit. At the end of the day, giving rightful credit doesn't just help you, it makes your creditor look good, too.

👊 SHimitate

Move a preposition and a noun, and let the games begin.

> YOU: "Given our first-quarter performance, I think it's important we devote more resources to marketing."
>
> BRO: "You, know, Bob—marketing did really well in Q1. We should spend more money there."
>
> YOU: "Yup. As I said three seconds ago, it makes sense to increase our marketing budget."
>
> BRO: "Blah blah blah—*my* recommendation is that we double down on our spend."

YOU: "I'm glad you're in agreement with me, *CHAD*. Since we're all on the same page here I'm gonna go ahead and let the marketing team know we'll be increasing their budgets."

Reach Clitoral Mass

Or: the distinctly *female* version of *critical mass*. One way to ensure that women are listened to *the first time* is to increase their numbers in the room: it makes them more likely to speak up—and they have more influence when they do. Start small: by supporting other women and backing up their ideas.

Take an Oath to Speak Up

SPEAK-UP COMPETISH

I, _____ , vow to speak up really fucking loud in meetings or when I'm pitching an idea, even if other people don't like it, because the research shows that as a woman, I am less likely to be heard from the get-go.

To make this delivery more memorable, I, _____, will speak clearly and slowly. I will stand up if it's appropriate and make eye contact with the person I most want to hear what I'm saying. These strategies may not block a dude who's purposely repeating what I say, but they will help me be heard the first time.

_____

X sign here

The Enemy:
THE MENSTRUHATER

"I remember the engineers trying
to decide how many tampons should
fly on a one-week flight; they
asked, 'Is one hundred the right
number?' No. That would not be
the right number."

—Astronaut Sally Ride, the
first American woman to go
into space

The Menstruhater assumes that any time a direct assertion comes out of a woman's mouth it *must* be "that time of the month"; that the tone of your voice couldn't possibly have anything to do with the *urgency* of a situation but that you must have forgotten to take your Midol that morning. The Menstruhater is Donald Trump to Megyn Kelly—who suggested that the Fox News anchor must have been "bleeding out of her whatever" because she dared ask about his verbal attacks on women. But he also goes as far back as the early days of space flight, when menstruation was part of the official NASA argument—in the 1960s—for why women shouldn't become astronauts. These days, he's also likely to emerge in the form of that mostly likable bro who comes up to you after a meeting—a meeting where you expressed displeasure with something—and asks, "Are you *OK*? You seemed really *upset*."

THE FIGHT MOVES

🤜 The Diss and Dismiss

Call the Menstruhater out. "Nope, PJ, I'm not on my period—but your sales reports look to be bleeding this company dry." "Oh wait, Sam, I'm confused. Do you mean *the time of the month when I conduct your performance review*?"

🤜 Keep Calm & Carry On

How many times have you watched a dude bang his keyboard, slam his phone, or scream at another colleague, and earn respect—while if a woman were to do the same, she'd be deemed insane? It's unfair, but it's real: men gain professional status when they act angry, viewed as "passionate" about the job, while women lose status. So take a deep breath keep an even tone. Speak deliberately. Your anger is valid—but channel it into strategic maneuvers. Don't give him an easy way to say, "See?"

🤜 Get Mad *and* Even

So a man who's angry is just "angry," while a woman who's angry is "hormonal," right? It isn't fair, but there is a way to hack the double standard, according to the professor Joan C. Williams, the author of *What Works for Women at Work*, who advises women to emphasize *why* they're upset. She provides a script: "If I look angry, it's because I am angry, and I'm angry because you have jeopardized [insert shared business goal here]." The idea is to show that you're not having a "chick fit"—somebody screwed up, and it's affecting the work.

IS THAT WOMAN ON HER PERIOD

ARE YOU HER TAMPON ?

↓

NO ?

↓

THEN IT'S NONE OF YOUR FUCKING BUSINESS

DOES THIS MEAN SHE'S ON HER PERIOD?

A FLOW CHART ABOUT FLOW

CRYING IN STAIRWELL

NOT SMILING

DIDN'T LAUGH AT YOUR JOKE

DIDN'T COME TO YOUR DJ SET

DESK COVERED IN SNACKS

DECLINED TO JOIN OFFICE FANTASY LEAGUE

WATCHING THE NOTEBOOK IN CUBICLE

NO EXCLAMATION POINT IN TEXT MESSAGE

MAYBE? 25% CHANCE? BUT PROBABLY NOT

The Enemy:
THE LACTHATER

The Lacthater is the colleague who views the mom on your team as preoccupied and unserious. He doesn't seem to know (or care) that, according to research, mothers are actually *more* ambitious than their childless colleagues, because he assumes that they are uncommitted (god forbid a woman commits to her family *and* her job). The Lacthater may not even realize he's made such assumptions—and women can be Lacthaters too—but the data prove this cognitive shortcut is real. Female job applicants with kids are 44 percent less likely to be hired than childless women with similar qualifications, while just three additional little words on a woman's résumé—"parent-teacher coordinator"—make her 79 percent less likely to be hired, half as likely to be promoted, offered an average of $11,000 less in salary and held to higher standards of punctuality. For black and Latina women that penalty is worse—and doubly problematic as women of color are more likely to be the breadwinners in their homes.

THE FIGHT MOVES

🤜 Mom on the Grind

Newsflash: being a mom is an *asset*. Studies have found that women with kids are actually *more* productive than those without, and they get even more productive the more kids they have (no time for nonsense!). Women with children are also more interested in being executives than women without. Whether you're a mom or not, make an effort to remind your higher-ups: nobody gets shit done like a mom.

🤜 Committed to the Job

Block a Lacthater by clearly emphasizing that *despite* caring for a small being, you're still committed to the job. Ask for a meeting to lay out your career goals post-maternity leave (assuming you have it) and make it clear that you're still the same ambitious employee (if, that is, you are). In one study of married parents applying for an engineering job, those who included a single sentence about being willing to make sacrifices for work were more likely to be hired. Sometimes it's as simple as saying it out loud.

🤜 Don't Make Assumptions

If you're on the other side: Don't simply *assume* that because a new mom leaves early she's not pulling her weight, and try not to penalize working parents if they have to adjust their schedules every now and then to deal with family stuff. What matters is that the work is getting done. If it is, then don't waste your time worrying about how it happens.

👊 Fight for Flex-Time

Research has found that more flexible hours, compressed workweeks, and more autonomy may actually make employees more productive (and happier) than the traditional nine to five—and it's certainly better for working parents. So if you're in charge: advocate for office policies that value getting work *done* over spending time in the office. And while you're at it, fight for parental leave policies—and encourage both genders to take them. If *every* parent took equal time off to care for their kids, this wouldn't be a "women's" problem.

👊 Fly Under the Radar

If you don't feel comfortable telling your boss you've got to step out to do something kid-related, see if you can come up with something else—and don't feel guilty about it. Try a doctor's appointment, or marking your shared-access calendar with a label like "offsite meeting" instead of "pick Kai up from daycare."

WILL I PUMP TODAY?

A Working Mother's Flowchart

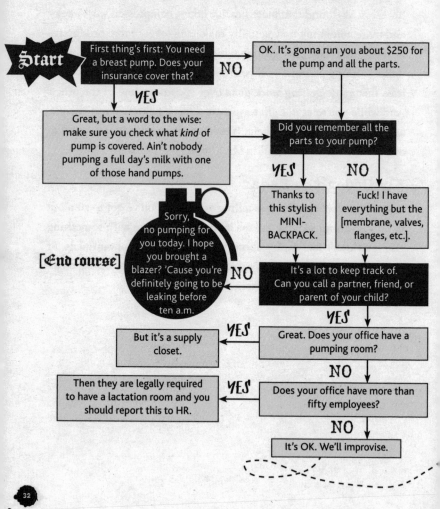

Start

First thing's first: You need a breast pump. Does your insurance cover that?

NO → OK. It's gonna run you about $250 for the pump and all the parts.

YES ↓

Great, but a word to the wise: make sure you check what *kind* of pump is covered. Ain't nobody pumping a full day's milk with one of those hand pumps.

Did you remember all the parts to your pump?

YES — Thanks to this stylish MINI-BACKPACK.

NO — Fuck! I have everything but the [membrane, valves, flanges, etc.].

It's a lot to keep track of. Can you call a partner, friend, or parent of your child?

NO → Sorry, no pumping for you today. I hope you brought a blazer? 'Cause you're definitely going to be leaking before ten a.m. **[End course]**

YES ↓

Great. Does your office have a pumping room?

YES → But it's a supply closet.

NO ↓

Does your office have more than fifty employees?

YES → Then they are legally required to have a lactation room and you should report this to HR.

NO ↓

It's OK. We'll improvise.

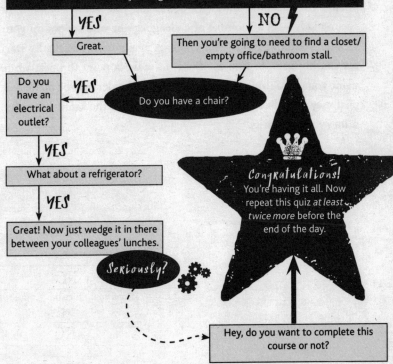

Do you have any of the following in or near your office?

- A LIBRARY. A McDonald's employee in Nebraska pumped here after her manager said she couldn't use the bathroom.
- A SHOWER STALL. This is where my friend Rosie pumps, at a major urban hospital.
- A SERVER ROOM. My friend Isolde, an employee of a public radio station, pumps here. She uses a Hawaiian lei on the doorknob to let people know not to enter.
- A CAR. But you might want to avoid red lights.

YES

Great.

NO

Then you're going to need to find a closet/empty office/bathroom stall.

Do you have an electrical outlet?

YES

Do you have a chair?

YES

What about a refrigerator?

YES

Great! Now just wedge it in there between your colleagues' lunches.

Seriously?

Congratulations! You're having it all. Now repeat this quiz *at least twice more* before the end of the day.

Hey, do you want to complete this course or not?

33

The Enemy:
THE UNDERMINE-HER

The Undermine-Her slowly chips away at your patience, and your reputation, by reducing you to your sex, your race, or your age. He acts comically aghast when you politely ask him not to interrupt ("So *sensitive,* jeez!") or loudly asks how "recess went" when your colleague with a toddler walks into a meeting late (and she was actually on the phone). He somehow thinks it's OK to call you "squirt," "kiddo," or "young lady"—in a roomful of colleagues—or who screws up your "ethnic" sounding name over and over again, until you finally start responding back to him as "Brad" to make a point (bro-iest white name you could think of on the spot). His behavior may be malicious, or it may be oblivious. Either way, the result is the same: he undermines your authority.

THE FIGHT MOVES

👊 Earmuffs

If it's a one- or two-time thing: ignore him. Like a kid brother pinching you until you react, some Undermine-Hers are looking for just that: a reaction. Don't give him the satisfaction.

👊 Get In His Head

It's easier to confront the Undermine-Her—or to plot your response— if you know where the behavior is stemming from. Is he jealous of your power? Does he mean well but is oblivious? Respond accordingly.

👊 Tell Him How It Is

If he's your supervisor, or a colleague you work with, then most likely it's in his best interest to make you look good. Explain that. "Chris, I'm trying to establish myself on our team, but I worry it undermines us when you refer to me as 'young lady.'" Or try the direct approach: "Geoff, it undermines what I'm trying to say when you call me 'honey.' Please stop."

👊 Bring the Heat

If he's simply an obnoxious, heckling colleague—and if undermining the Undermine-Her isn't going to hurt *you*—then toss the politeness. "My 'pretty little head' outsold your sales figures by three last month. But *thanks for asking*." "I think by 'young lady' you mean 'woman in charge.' That's how we refer to female leaders nowadays."

The Enemy:
THE FRAT SOCIAL CHAIR

At Kleiner Perkins, the Silicon Valley investment firm that once employed (and was later sued by) Ellen Pao, the Frat Social Chair came in the form of a partner who organized a company-wide ski trip from which women were excluded and, later, a men-only dinner with former vice president Al Gore because, as the partner said, the women would "kill the buzz." While not all Social Chairs are so overt, there are plenty who are clueless: organizing dinner for a half-dozen employees at a conference but forgetting to invite the only woman present; heading to the bar with his buddies after work and not bothering to tell the only woman on the team. The point of "social events" is to bond, team-build, break the ice—but the Frat Social Chair ends up doing the opposite: making people feel excluded (and depriving them of valuable face time).

COMPANY EVENT CALENDAR

MON	TUE	WED	THU
10 AM MEETING	10 AM MEETING	10 AM BREAKFAST	10 AM MEETING
1 PM LUNCH	2 PM ~~SQUASH~~	11 AM MEETING	1 PM
4 PM ~~BEER PONG~~	SCREENING OF THE NOTEBOOK	7 PM ~~STRIP CLUB~~ VEGAN COOKING CLASS	*AFTERNOON NAP* ♡
PERIOD ↑ SEMINAR			

THE FIGHT MOVES

👊 Shevent Planner

Take a gander at the upcoming events calendar (if it exists). Does it involve beer pong? A trip to the shooting range? Does the largest group of employees want to take part in these things? No? Try the direct approach: "How 'bout we do the next offsite at ___. I think it would encourage more women to show up." Or the indirect: "Oooh! Check out this awesome ___. We should consider this for our next offsite!" Oh, and small piece of duh advice: if you're in a field with a notorious gender imbalance, at a company that's being sued for sexism, perhaps throwing a fraternity-themed party isn't the best idea. (I'm looking at you, Twitter.)

👊 Open Invitation

Invite yourself—and consider forcing yourself to go. Sarah, a thirty-three-year-old lawyer in Philadelphia, noticed that all the male partners at her firm would bro-down talking about the company fantasy football team. She wasn't invited into the league, so she invited herself—and furiously started tracking her teams. "They all looked at me like I was crazy, but they couldn't say no," she said. It was worth it: she got valuable face time with her bosses—and she also won.

Attendance Is Womandatory

Working hard is great, but don't underestimate the value of *relation-ships*. Case in point: A young woman named Adina, a junior in college, was interning at an investment firm over the summer. She stayed late most nights working while her male cubemate went out for drinks with the partners. While she sat late in an empty office, he was socializing with the people in charge. No, maybe you don't want to go to some bro-y happy hour. Maybe you don't even drink. Order a seltzer with a lime and bring a female friend. The more women go to these outings the less bro-y they'll become.

Squad Goals

Throw your own outing. Yep, when the guys are heading off for lunchtime squash, you'll already be having fun with your female colleagues at the local [fill in your own blank]. Soon the dudes will be begging to join your group. If they're not, invite them! The only thing guys (well, some guys) like better than hanging out with one another is hanging out with women.

WORKING WITH A VAGINA

& A MALE BOSS

The Enemy:
THE HOVERER

Like clockwork, he would appear at my desk—the boss who could come up with any number of reasons to talk to me about politics, the weather, sports. As far as I could tell his main objective was to casually stare down my shirt. The Hoverer is a neutered version of the creepy *Mad Men*-era ass grabber that your mother and grandmother had to contend with—and while he may not *actually* cross a line, he's always about two minutes away from asking you out (and if it weren't for HR departments and sexual harassment policies, he probably would). Either way, he makes you uncomfortable—and you want him to scram.

THE FIGHT MOVES

🤜 Wall Yourself Off

A 1967 advice book for working women, *Secretaries on the Spot,* tells the story of a woman whose boss "had a habit of leaning over her desk" and placing "his arm around her shoulder." She casually moved her desk against a wall so that it could only be approached from one side—and then, she stacked papers high so that he couldn't reach her.

🤜 Call For Backup

Chances are if this person is creeping you out, other people are feeling creeped out too, and there is always more power in approaching a problem as a group. Have others noticed the hovering? Can you talk about it? If there's a collective no-tolerance policy, no one can be (or feel) singled out.

🤜 The Brush Off

Avoid unnecessary contact. When the Hoverer is in the vicinity, do not make yourself available for conversation. Plug in headphones. Look away. Call your own voicemail. If you must engage, keep your conversations short and say you have to get back to work.

🤜 See Something, Say Something

Keep a record of each and every creepy interaction, with the time, date, and circumstances. If it continues, report him to HR—or to the most senior person you work with.

The Enemy:
THE SLACKLUSTER

George would show up late to the office and obviously stoned. Then he'd spend roughly six hours inputting small amounts of information into an Excel spreadsheet and carefully planning his lunch order. Around three p.m., he'd casually dip out. Nobody knew where he went, and none of the bosses really noticed, but all of the junior employees timed his return. He was twenty-five, six foot two, with an in-between shag haircut that screamed *Dude, just decide which length you want to go with*. (He did have great food recommendations, though.) George was a Slackluster: that guy who seems to get away with doing jack shit yet somehow manages to keep his job and even get promoted (we call that "failing up"). The Slackluster can take on various forms, but all Slacklusters have one thing in common: they feed on blind confidence, growing stronger because most of us have trouble discerning *competence* (actually being good at your job) from *confidence* (acting like you're good at it). Add to that the fact that men are more likely to perceive their work as better than it is (while women perceive their work to be worse), and the Slackluster makes an art out of doing nothing, while we quietly watch him rise.

THE FIGHT MOVES

🤛 Diagnose

Before you go HAM on his ass, make sure you're diagnosing correctly. It *is* possible—unlikely, but possible—that what you perceive as slacking might actually just be hyperefficiency. Observe him and find out. And, hey, if he really is able to finish all his work *and* get in a few rounds of Candy Crush during the day, then you might stand to borrow a few of his tricks.

🤛 Don't Cover for Him

No, you don't have to be a snitch, but realize that the Slackluster gets away with doing nothing in part because nobody calls him out on it. If the Slackluster tries to delegate to you (Slacklusters are great at delegating work they don't want to do themselves), don't fall for it. If a boss comes looking for him, don't say you "think he went to grab lunch" when you know he's actually in the back smoking a J. The Slackluster's biggest dependency is on nonconfrontational colleagues.

🤛 Attack His Slack

If you have to work with this person, and he has some redeeming qualities that make him even *minimally* indispensable, then see if it's worth coming up with a system to make him more efficient. Maybe he needs frequent and continuous deadlines. Maybe he's just a complete space cadet. Stay on him, and ask to be updated regularly while his work is in progress.

👊 Bring it to the Boss

Determine how (and whether) the Slackluster is affecting *your* job. If he's just annoying, try to tune him out—you've got bigger battles to wage. If he's making your life impossible, if he's jeopardizing *your* work, then consider speaking up (to him or directly to your boss). If you choose the latter, come prepared. You need a concrete and non-speculative record of Slackluster misconduct, and for delivering that news, there's power in numbers: a solo tattle tale is just a snitch, but a group of people pointing out inefficiencies is in the company's best interest.

DO YOU KNOW YOUR SPORTS LINGO?

Intercepting The Office Jock

 The Office Jock congratulates you on your "slam dunk" presentation, suggests the team focus on "moving the chains," and offers up a strategy for "pulling the trigger." He comes in the form of Supreme Court justice John Roberts, who, during his nomination hearing, testified that "my job is to call balls and strikes and not to pitch or bat." He's even *Barack Obama,* who when asked to articulate the principles of his foreign policy plan said, "You hit singles, you hit doubles; every once in a while we may be able to hit a home run."

The Office Jock can be a woman, too: let's not make the mistake of assuming *only* men like sports (participating in athletics, in fact, helps *breed* female leaders). But it is women, not men, who report feeling excluded by that bro-y language, and in turn feel like they must cultivate it in order to fit in.

If we play our FFC cards right, boss ladies everywhere will soon put the Office Jock in his rightful place: *the penalty box* (heh). But until then, here's a quiz to help you beat him at his own game

Match the Phrase with the Definition

1. Blocking and Tackling

A. Using your body to physically keep someone from entering your office or cubicle
B. When you try to go to a questionable website and your company's firewall prevents it
C. Handling the day-to-day low-level stuff

2. Move the Goalposts

A. Pulling someone's chair out from under him as he's about to sit down
B. Changing the stated goal of a project after the project has already started
C. Rearranging someone's desk while she's on vacation

3. Slam Dunk

A. When you drop your pen into your cup of coffee
B. An impromptu in-office poetry reading
C. Something so obviously good and easy no one could argue with it

4. Call an Audible

A. Calling the IT department to connect your computer to a projector during a presentation
B. Changing plans at the last moment
C. Calling a 900 number from your work phone

5. Tee It Up

A. Making sure everyone wears matching T-shirts on casual Friday
B. When someone asks you if you'd like some tea and you want to reply in the affirmative
C. Getting something ready so that it's easy for someone else to take over

6. Pole Position

A. Being in the best possible situation relative to competitors
B. When someone gets too drunk at the holiday party and wilds out on the dance floor
C. The seat or office that's closest to the pole in a firehouse

7. Hail Mary

A. A last-ditch attempt at something that has only a small chance of succeeding
B. What you drink to get through the morning after a really late night out
C. Having a group prayer before a team meeting

ANSWER KEY

1.	C	4.	B	7.	A
2.	B	5.	C		
3.	C	6.	A		

Part Two

KNOW THYSELF

Female
SELF-SABOTAGE

I t's a strange feeling to believe, at your very core, that you're good at something—and yet simultaneously doubt that very thing is ture. I never remembered feeling that way in high school, or even college. But six months into my first job, doubt crept in and became a constant voice in the back of my head. Soon, it seemed to be taking over.

It began as I watched the guys in my intern class get promoted into staff writing jobs, while I was still a part-time temp, babysitting for my editor's kid on weekends and working nights at a bar. It continued after I was hired on staff and was settling into my career, even as I outpaced those same guys. Sometimes it was just a quiet question: *Are you good enough?* But it caused me to stumble over my words in meetings, certain I sounded like an idiot, or offer to grab the coffee or take the notes so that at least I'd be visibly contributing.

I was lucky, in a way: I knew that I was not alone, because back with the Club, others were feeling versions of this too. It came up at one particular meeting, where Shauna, a spunky television writer, described pitching her first pilot to a network. The network told her they loved it—the only problem was that they needed something just a bit more "male" for their audience (she had a female lead). Shauna was so shocked she said nothing, at a loss for the witty retort she always had waiting in reserve. She wondered if they were joking, if they'd actually said that out loud. When it was clear they weren't, she politely thanked them and left. She spent the next months angry at herself for not fighting harder for her script.

The problem manifested differently for others. Amanda, a research assistant at a nonprofit, shared a story of going in for her performance review and being told she was doing an *amazing* job—which would have conceivably been followed by a salary bump had she not literally interrupted her boss to say, "If you're happy then that's *all the raise I need*." (Yes, really.) Nell, a stand-up comic, remarked that she'd felt so awkward receiving praise from another comic she admired, after a recent set, that she pretended to get a phone call. Alicia, another one of the women, joked that she was thinking about cutting her long hair into a bob (or pinning it back each day) because she got so nervous when she spoke in meetings that she had a habit of twirling it.

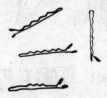

What was *up* with all of us? Why couldn't we voice our ideas with conviction or accept praise or stand to be the center of attention? We had announced a rule early on in our meetings: you could complain as much as you wanted, but that you also had to brag. If not for yourself, then on behalf of somebody else. But we were doing the opposite of bragging. Instead of a fight club our dinner had become a forlorn group therapy session: sad, self-sabotaging feminists' edition.

In 1963 Betty Friedan published *The Feminine Mystique,* in which she described a feeling that so many women of her era experienced but

none had spoken out loud: it was an unease, a sense of emptiness, a feeling that—though they had suburban homes and shiny dishwashers and children and husbands (all the things a woman could want!)—there was something . . . *missing*. It was a white, upper-middle-class problem primarily: not everybody had the luxury of such emptiness. Nevertheless, it began a revolution. Friedan called it "the problem that has no name."

Perhaps today's problem without a name emerges from the remnants of that feeling. The emptiness is gone—women are allowed to have careers—but it's replaced by a sense that we still don't deserve to be there. It plays out in ways big and small: It's that little voice of self-doubt that chips away at your confidence; the feeling that even when you get the promotion, you're undeserving, unprepared, likely to screw it all up; or the sense that one tiny mistake means that you should *probably just give up, you weren't cut out for this job*. It's modesty in the face of a compliment. Saying yes when you really want to say no. Pretzeling up our legs and bodies so as not to take up too much space. Putting your head down and working hard, with the good-faith assumption that you will be recognized for your ultraquiet diligence.

Why do we feel so conflicted? History, for one—a product of centuries of being viewed as the "weaker sex," of being told we don't belong, and then having that feeling saturate our psyches, down to our bones. It's confusion: at being told we can accomplish *whatever we put our minds to!*—then realizing that it isn't always true (and not because of merit). But it's also pressure: to make good on the groundwork laid for us by generations before us. To be flawless, to be perfect, and to do it without visible effort—knowing that our missteps will be noticed more and remembered longer than those of our male peers.*

Everyone gets in their own way sometimes—men too. What is essential is recognizing when it's happening and becoming aware of it so that we can find a workaround—or talk ourselves off the ledge.

---

* FACT.

The Saboteur:
THE OFFICE MOM

She volunteers to organize the Thanksgiving food drive, runs the company's mentorship program, and stays late to plan the company holiday party even when she's already got too much on her plate. (Sometimes you can *literally* find her cleaning the break-room kitchen.) She's the Office Mom, and you've probably met her: study after study has found that women take on the lion's share of so-called office housework and often don't receive credit for it. This is even more pronounced for black and Latina women, who regularly report being pressured by male colleagues to do more administrative work like organizing meetings and filling out forms. Now sure, an Office Mom might not *mind* doing the work . . . sometimes. But that's not the point. The point is that this type of work won't benefit her professionally in the same way it benefits men.* In fact, men who do the same amount of "office housework" as women are more likely to be recommended for promotions, important projects, raises, and bonuses.

---

* Yup. A study out of New York University found that a man who offered to stay late at work was evaluated 14 percent more favorably than a woman who offered the same—yet when both the man and woman declined to help out, the woman was docked for it, given a 12 percent lower rating.

THE FIGHT MOVES

🤜 Mother-Ducker

Duck as many "motherly" tasks as possible. That means notes, mailings, lunch orders, party planning, or anything else you know a man wouldn't be asked to do. If you feel like you're the one who always gets assigned these tasks, and you have power, delegate them to others. If you don't have the power, ask others to chip in (or the assigner if they would mind asking *Joe* to help because you've got "a lot on your plate"). Evaluate the situation and consider saying no or asking for something in return. Remember: if you act like a volunteer, chances are you'll be treated like one.

🤜 Rock the Clock

Clock the amount of time you spend on these tasks—keeping in mind that it isn't the type of work that's going to get you noticed (at least not in the way that's going to make your boss think you deserve a promotion). Even if you never need to use it, keeping a written record will allow you to explain—should the occasion arise—precisely how much time you spend on tasks that may be benefitting the company but aren't benefitting your career.

PDA (Public Display of Additional Work)

Make sure the work you're doing, even the small stuff, is being *seen* by those who need to see it (in other words, don't fall into the "a tree fell in the woods" trap). Studies show that when men offer to help they're more likely to act out the help in *public*—making sure they are observed in the act—while women do so quietly behind the scenes. So, sure, you don't mind folding napkins after your shift ends, or making copies for an early morning meeting. Just be sure to do it in a high-traffic area where everyone will see you putting in the extra time. And if you notice a female colleague taking on more than her share, commend her out loud to help her get some credit.

A System to Assist Him

Set up a rotation system, so you don't get stuck with the "mother" load of menial tasks. Whether it's a spreadsheet, a calendar invite, or drawing names out of a bowl, if you have the power to set up a system, use it—and if you don't, make a point to notice who's taking on more than her fair share of the work (and maybe even offer to help).

The Saboteur:
THE CREDIT DEFAULTER

Ask a man to explain his success and he'll point to his innate qualities and skill. But ask a woman and she'll attribute it to things like "hard work," "help from others," or "luck." The Credit Defaulter knows there's no "I" in team—but she often forgets that there is an "I" in "I deserve a raise," "I led that project," or "I want a promotion." A product of centuries (if not millennia) spent denying women credit for their achievements (see the Bropropriator, page 11)—and telling them they must be "modest" in the process—the Credit Defaulter is hesitant to talk about her achievements and even lowballs her expertise relative to men. The Credit Defaulter makes the mistake of playing the team *too much* and not taking credit even when it's deserved—undermining her competence.

THE FIGHT MOVES

👊 Drop the "Grateful" Cred

You know this kind of credit: being "grateful" for all the help you had from your team, instead of simply accepting credit. Women already give away more credit than is necessary—or even true—to their colleagues ("I couldn't have done it without Sam!"), in some instances even pointing to their own negative qualities in order to deflect. The first step in not letting others take credit for your work is not giving it away. Don't give out credit like it's candy.

👊 Take Credit Where It's Due

Make sure your *individual* contribution is known when working on team projects—especially if there are men on your team. Research has found that while women are given roughly equal credit for work they perform alone or with other women, when they work with men they are at a disadvantage—because the men receive the default credit for the team's work.

👊 Accept Praise

Employ the following radical yet simple act of self-care: saying "Thank you" next time somebody compliments you on your work.

> **BOSS:** Great work on your presentation today!
> **YOU:** Thanks! ~~But it was really all Harold~~.

> **BOSS:** Nice work on that proposal; I know a lot went into it.
> **YOU:** Thank you. ~~It was really no big deal.~~ (May add: I worked really hard on it.)

COWORKER: Congrats on the promotion.

YOU: Thanks. ~~I got really lucky.~~

✊ Selective Framing

There's a scene in *Annie Hall*, the Woody Allen film, in which Allen's character, Alvy, tries to figure out why his relationship with Diane Keaton (Annie) has failed. Each is sitting in a therapist's chair; asked how often they have sex. "Hardly ever. Maybe three times a week," says Alvy. "Constantly. I'd say three times a week," says Annie. It's a perfect conveyance of how important *framing* is to any delivery of information. Here's how this plays out in the workplace:

EMPLOYER: Tell me about your experience.

STEVE: I've already had six months of experience, and—

WILLA: I've only had six months of experience, but—

Don't be Willa!

DARLING, JUST FUCKING OWN IT: AN FFC MAD LIB

I, _____ [your name], will start taking credit for my achievements.

I, _____ [your name], did not "get lucky." It was not _____ [choose one: "nothing," "no big deal," "really all Kevin"].

My _____ [work-related task] was _____ [affirmative adjective]. I worked _____ [adverb followed by "fucking"] hard on it.

_____ [first-person singular pronoun] could not have done it without the help of _____ [names of others who deserve credit], and _____ [first-person singular pronoun] am really proud of what _____ [first person plural pronoun] accomplished.

_____ [first-person singular pronoun] am _____ [affirmative adjective], _____ [affirmative adjective], and _____ [affirmative adjective].

I am a_____ [female version of king].

The Saboteur:
THE DOORMAT

She is afraid to say no, even when she wants to, and ends up overworked and exhausted as a result—placing the needs of others above her own. The Doormat differs from the Office Mom in that she's not simply being tasked with taking on the mothering role, it's that she's being relied upon to take on *everything*—and unfortunately for her, the remedy isn't as simple as saying no more often. The Doormat isn't simply a pushover, though she likely knows that there's an implicit *expectation* that she says yes because she's female—communal! agreeable! helpful!—and she's right. When men say no to extra work, we understand (he must be busy!), but when women decline they are penalized: they receive worse performance evaluations, fewer recommendations for promotions, and are considered less likable by their peers. So how do you say no without incurring the penalty—or, at least, decide when the ding is worth it?

THE FIGHT MOVES

👊 Know Your Rung

Assess your place on the overall ladder. Are you an intern? An assistant? Is it your job to put in extra hours and legwork? Yes? Then it's probably not an awesome idea to start refusing to do so. In either case, assess your rung on the ladder—and who's doing the asking. Is it a senior colleague, or the fellow intern in the cubicle next to you? As with all the guidance in this book, trust your instincts—and common sense.

👊 Assess the Cost

Weigh the task—or the "opportunity," as it may be—before you commit. How time-consuming is it? What will you get out of it? Is it an appropriate task to be asked of you—e.g., please help me fact-check this document—or are you a manager being asked to pick up your boss's dry-cleaning? Consider all of this in context: Do you like, respect, or work directly for the person asking? Does this person *always* ask for help, or is this a rare instance? Will they reciprocate? Do you actually *enjoy* doing this task? None of these are earth-shattering questions, but it's worth being strategic. If reviewing someone's report will put you in their good graces, then do it. Saying yes is not a bad thing necessarily, but keep in mind that people often do it simply out of obligation.

Just Say No

Try to separate refusal from rejection. Both women and men tend to feel guilty when they have to say no, but women feel *more* guilty about it. Remind yourself that you are saying no to the *request,* not the person. Think about the costs associated with *not* saying no—such as less time spent on more important work, on fulfilling work, or just getting out of the office. Remember: You can't make everyone happy all the time. If you are employed, and not a volunteer helping sick children, nice is not your number-one priority.

Underpromise, Overdeliver

Research shows that we expect women to say yes more frequently than men (that patriarchy, man!). But studies also show that those asking for the help actually *underestimate* how likely a person is to say yes (in other words: they may be more prepared to receive a "no" than you are to give it). In some circumstances, it's safe to assume that the other party isn't expecting you to say yes as much as you may think they are.

Quid Pro Quo

It's not just not saying no that causes inequity—it's not asking for something in return when you do. As you're weighing the decision about whether to complete the task, ask yourself: What's in it for me?

How to Say no

Fig. 1

Fig. 2

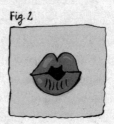

SITUATION: You really don't have time
INSTEAD OF: "There's no way I can do that."
SAY (IF IT'S YOUR BOSS): "I'm swamped right now but I'd like to help. Can you help me prioritize?"
SAY (IF IT'S A COLLEAGUE): "What's your timeline? I have a couple of other things on my plate at the moment."

SITUATION: You disagree with the ask
INSTEAD OF: "I don't think that will work."
SAY: "I have another idea to throw out . . ."

SITUATION: You don't want to do it (but don't have a good excuse)
INSTEAD OF: "No"
SAY (IF IT'S A COLLEAGUE): "Sure, I'd be happy to. Do you mind doing [something equally awful/tedious/horrifying] for me in return?"

SITUATION: The ask is ridiculous/inappropriate
INSTEAD OF: "Fuck. You."
SAY: "Unfortunately, I can't." (Then stop yourself from explaining further. That whole justification thing won't work for assholes anyway.)

The Saboteur:
THE CONTORTIONIST

She's the student who curls her legs beneath her in her seat, crouches her body around them, and raises her hand nervously, as if she's trying not to take up too much room. Why is she all pretzeled up like this? The theories span the gamut: she's making herself small; she's physically protecting her organs; she's trying to appear unthreatening. What's clear is that she's *female*—men don't contort their bodies to appear small—and that she's undermining herself in the process. Research has found that up to 93 percent of the information we infer from others is nonverbal, meaning the old adge that it's not *what* you say, but *how* you say it is true.* The Contortionist may say the smartest thing in the room, but we'll be too busy noticing the weakness of her rubber limbs to hear it.

---

* In one study of 185 venture capital pitches, Boston College doctoral student Lakshmi Balachandra found that things like "calmness," "eye contact," and "lack of awkwardness"—in other words, charisma—were actually better indicators of who received funding than the actual content of the pitches.

THE FIGHT MOVES

Size Matters

Be as big as you are. Sit up straight, stand tall, clench your fist to make a point, put your feet flat on the floor, and bring a sweater if you're cold, so you're not curling yourself up in a shawl. Harvard professor Amy Cuddy advises her female students to raise their adjustable classroom chairs as high as possible while still keeping their feet on the floor (let's avoid the dangling little girl legs) and says that many have reported it to be an effective tool in job interviews. Conveying authority through body language is a great tool for women, in part because it tends not to carry the same negative implications as so many of our other assertive actions.

Queen of Prop

Use objects as props to stop yourself from fidgeting while you're speaking: a pen, a mug, anything else that's going to occupy your hands and prevent you from messing with your hair and playing with your jewelry while you're speaking. Also try "steepling": pressing the tips of your fingers together in front of your chest, with your palms facing each other—so the result looks like a steeple and projects confidence.

👊 Womanspread

Learn to take up space. Really, force yourself to do it: women tend to occupy less space in public than men, holding their legs closer together and keeping their arms closer to their bodies. Try a manspread—stick out your shoe from underneath your desk like you're about to trip someone (but, uh, don't actually do it). Pretend there is a ruler against your back so you stand up straight—it's likely to make others see you as more confident. If you're feeling really advanced, attempt the Bro Lean: chair teetering back, hands clasped behind your head, feet up on desk. (Just don't turn the bro lean into a bro crash.)

👊 Copycat

Model your body language (and your *actual* language, for that matter) on the most confident person in the room—or the one you want to impress. Does she get out of her seat when she's speaking to the room? Then try it. If you're having trouble keeping people's attention during a (casual) meeting, it's a way to keep all eyes on you.

BE A POWER POSER

Plenty of people have rituals before giving a big speech. They talk to themselves in the mirror. They pop a Xanax. They listen to Bach, or Beethoven, or Janet Jackson ("Rhythm Nation," obvs). When I'm about to go onstage, I hold a coffee mug to keep my hands from trembling, and then I take it with me—it gives me a caffeine boost while solving the problem of not knowing where to put my hands.

If you're my friend Sally Kohn, though—a six-foot-one progressive lesbian about to debate politics with a conservative white guy on Fox News—you do the following: Walk into the bathroom, or a hallway, or an alleyway—basically anywhere you can be alone for a while. Spread your feet, straighten your back, and put your hands on your hips. Tilt your chin up, take a deep breath, and then

HIGH POWER POSES

stay cemented in this position for a full two minutes—at which point your testosterone levels rise and your cortisone levels drop, making you immediately more confident and less anxious. Then straighten your shirt, flip your hair, and walk on set like a boss-ass bitch. Easy, right?

Sally learned this trick from Amy Cuddy, the Harvard psychologist whose TED Talk on the "power pose" has spawned a global following. The allure of Cuddy's work lies in the fact that it is so easy to implement. There are "high power" poses—those that increase your confidence—and "low power" poses, or those that reduce it. Now: channel your inner Wonder Woman and strike a power pose.

LOW POWER POSES

SMARTPHONE HUNCH

TIMID STUDENT

PRETZEL LEGS

SLIP'N'SLIDE

The Saboteur:
THE PERMASSISTANT

The head of a New York vocational school once advised his female students *not* to learn shorthand—because, as he put it, the "bright girl" who took dictation was "such a treasure" that she might find herself permanently stuck by her boss's side, stenographer's notebook in hand.

The steno pad has gone the way of the rotary phone, thank god, but the Permassistant remains. She's so good at keeping her boss's life in check that he can't live without her. She struggles to get her colleagues to see her as anything but the office admin. She is patient and loyal, and she hopes—no, assumes—that good work will help her rise up. But somehow she finds herself stuck. There is such a thing as being *too* good at your assistant job—at least when it's one you don't want to keep.

> "Don't let them stick you with taking notes in meetings. Otherwise you'll be transcribing far into the afternoon while the other people are getting on with what the meeting was called about."
> —*Cosmopolitan* editor Helen Gurley Brown

THE FIGHT MOVES

🤜 Show 'n' Grow

Pick up other assignments that allow you to stretch your skills; if it's an option, take on "extra credit" or outside work that might help you get noticed. If you get tapped for a high-visibility project, say yes. The office isn't like dating—but sometimes it is. They might not notice you until somebody else does.

🤜 Two Legit Then Quit

A twenty-three-year-old assistant at a talent agency in Los Angeles told me he made a point of discussing with his boss during his interview that while he was happy to put in long hours and work hard, he was also interested in advancing his career and had set goals as part of a two-year plan for himself. A two-year plan may not always be realistic, so deploy this fight move with care—but the point is to make clear from the outset that you're interested in growth.

🤜 Move Up or Move On

Set a deadline for yourself. If, like the man above, you've made a two-year plan and it doesn't feel like you're on track to reach it, ask for a meeting to discuss your ambitions and what you could be doing better to achieve them. Patience is a virtue, but so is knowing when to leave.

TIME TO OPEN A "FUCK-OFF FUND"

Tess McGill
1 Working Girl Way
New York, NY 00123

055

DATE 9/6/16

PAY TO THE
ORDER OF FUCK-OFF FUND | $ 87.00

SOME BANK

MEMO CAN'T STAND ANOTHER FUCKING MINUTE

⊥:555555555⊥: 5555555555⊪5555

It's an emergency fund for when you can no longer deal—in a job, a relationship, a living situation, or otherwise. Coined by the writer Paulette Perhach—who calls the Fuck-Off Fund a form of "financial self-defense"—your Fuck-Off Fund needn't start huge. Maybe it's a small sum put away each paycheck that over time adds up; perhaps it's just a few dollars when you can afford it. Whatever you can muster together, the idea is proactively saving money when and where you can because we all know that shit happens—especially at the start of a career. Also useful in cases of relationship meltdowns, creepy bosses, delinquent roommates, and workplaces in which you literally can't stand to spend another fucking minute.

The Saboteur:
SHE PUTS THE SHHH IN SHEEPISH

OKAY I NEED THIS

You can find this girl in the classroom—hesitantly raising her hand, only for a moment, before pulling it back down because she isn't 100 percent sure of the answer. You can find her in the office, speaking quietly from behind a desk, fearful that her voice will be perceived as *too loud* if she speaks up, or cowering in the conference room, reluctantly pitching an idea, then worrying that she went on for too long. Women are more likely than men to receive the feedback that they "don't speak up" in meetings, and the more outnumbered they are by men in a room, the less they speak. This behavior is a response, of course: to constant interruptions (see the Manterrupter, page 7), to fearing we'll come off as self-serving (see the Humble Bragger, page 79), to the fact that female experts have less *influence* in mixed-sex groups, to the fear of being wrong—and knowing we'll be judged more harshly if we are. But the end result is not having our ideas heard.

THE FIGHT MOVES

👊 No More Secrets

Know that this habit develops over a lifetime. It goes all the way back to preschool, where girls typically have a close friend or two with whom to whisper secrets—whereas boys have groups of friends with whom they play and shout commands. No huge surprise, then, that those boys grow up to be men who feel comfortable talking in large groups—shouting out answers—while women still favor one-on-one interactions or smaller group dynamics.

👊 Don't Lean—Jump

. . . Into the conversation. A *Harvard Business Review* study found that while men speak conversationally in meetings, women preferred to be more formal (and prepared). But the reality is that you can't always plot the perfect moment to speak—sometimes you just have to jump in. One friend, an editor at a magazine, forces herself to pitch two ideas per meeting and gives herself half credit for each time she weighs in on somebody else's ideas. Another woman I know makes a point of asking questions—targeted ones—because she finds it to be an easier way to speak spontaneously.

👊 Pre-Meet

Research has found that while women are highly *efficient* in office meetings—making effective use of time—men are more likely to spend time connecting with one another *beforehand* to test their ideas (and garner support). Get in on the meetings before the meetings, even if it's simply by showing up early and talking about your idea to whoever might listen. It can help you build allies, and you'll feel more prepared and supported when it's your turn to talk.

Speak Easy

I promise, even if you feel like you're blabbing—or even if you feel like *she* is blabbing—the actual amount of time spent speaking is probably less than you think. That's because, in mixed-gender groups, women are perceived as talking more than they actually do; their contributions are viewed as "equally balanced" when they actually talk 25 percent of the time or less, and are perceived as "dominating the conversation" when they speak just 25 to 50 percent of the time. It's a chicken and egg situation, of course: to speak up more while simultaneously changing the perception that we're speaking too much. But once every woman in the room is talking, it will just be *normal*.

Keep the Balance

Make your meetings more gender balanced—which will encourage women to speak up. Notice how much time the men and women on your teams spend talking, and encourage quieter employees to contribute. President Obama is known for calling on the quietest person in the room in meetings—why don't you try it, too?

YES BRAG
BE PROUD OF
YOURSELF &
YOUR ACHIEVEMENTS

BRAGGING!
IS ALLOWED!
USE THE
WORD

HELLO I'M
BRAGGING

THIS IS HOW: BE OPEN
AND HONEST | self-improvement

WE

FOR
TEAM

NOT

NOT TOO Humble .. ME ME ME ME
ME ME ME ME

The Saboteur:
THE HUMBLE BRAGGER

She's #blessed to have been granted a full scholarship, "grateful" (and "surprised!") to have been promoted, and feels #lucky—not *proud*—to have won a prestigious award. What she's *trying* to do is inform the world of her achievements—or in other words, self-promote. And why shouldn't she? She's proud of them. The problem with the Humble Bragger is that she hesitates to brag directly, instead masking her pride in faux humility. Why? She may not even be conscious of it, but the Humble Bragger knows that nobody likes a woman who boasts; she doesn't want to be viewed as cocky or immodest. But she also knows that too much awww-shucks modesty will undermine her. And so she's come up with a system: to brag but not brag, to promote without promoting, to attribute her accomplishments to #luck—so that we still like her. Which might be OK if it worked—but it doesn't.

THE FIGHT MOVES

Bag the Humblebrag

Narcissism may look bad, but insincerity looks worse: Not only does it make you less likable than outright bragging, but it's also ineffective—viewed as both obnoxious *and* inauthentic. But there is a way to brag that isn't self-promoting, isn't *necessarily* insincere, and won't get you docked for boasting: bragging in service of somebody else. So explain how awesome that thing you did was—and then explain how it helped others (your team, your company).

Don't Deprecate

One study found that people who bragged openly ("I'm the life of the party") were actually more likable than those who made self-deprecating claims ("I'm *never* the life of the party"). Women are deprecated enough already. Leave the self-deprecation to the men who can afford it.

Just the Facts

State facts, not opinions, when you're talking about yourself. It's a lot harder to accuse someone—or perceive someone—as bragging when they're stating something indisputable. As in, "I programmed 79,387 lines of code this month" *not* "I'm a really good programmer." While you're at it, try to frame your accomplishments in a way that compare you to you—not you to somebody else. So: "I programmed 79,387 lines of code, which is 10,000 more lines than I programmed last quarter" *not* "I programmed 79,387 lines of code, which is 10,000 more than Sasha over there." Again: science.

👊 Find a Boast Bitch

She's your female hype man. She boasts for you, you boast for her, boasting for each other makes you both look better, yet neither of you is perceived as bragging about yourself. And no, I'm not making this up: research shows that having someone boast on your behalf is effective even if it's clear that person is biased (like your mom). And if you're in the boasting position? That's great, too. It makes you look like a team player. Plus, isn't it always easier to boast on someone else's behalf, anyway?

---

boast bitch / n.
She and you have an unspoken agreement: she boasts
for you, you boast for her. Other duties include
memorizing your coffee order, complete honesty in
dressing rooms.

The Saboteur:
THE EVER-FAITHFUL

"It's not really about asking for a raise," said Satya Nadella, the CEO of Microsoft, "but knowing and having *faith* that the system will give you the *right* raise." Nadella was speaking to a crowd of women at the Grace Hopper Convention, which celebrates women in tech. The audience sat stunned. Um ... *have faith?*

The workplace isn't a convent, or even a Scientology center. Last time I checked, faith wasn't paying the bills or buying your next round. And yet the Ever-Faithful is real: that person who believes that by putting her head down and doing a great job, by being loyal to the company, by simply having *faith* in the system, she will succeed. She's the employee who doesn't pursue another job offer because she wants to show her commitment but then never gets that promotion she was hoping for. The merit system *can* work. But let's be clear: there is no divine providence in the workplace. You get only what you ask for.

THE FIGHT MOVES

👊 Loyalty Won't Pay Your Rent

... And yet women are less likely to leave a job after a few years than men. Sure, it's easy to think of reasons why you should stay: maybe you've watched the business grow, maybe you love your boss, maybe you've made great friends—and maybe you feel guilty. Don't. If you really do have a great boss, then she or he should be invested in helping you be happy.

👊 Ask for What You Want

Not the neutered, self-compromised version you think you can get. People—especially women—often don't ask for what they want, which is one reason why the wage gap (and many other things) still exist. Just *consider* asking for what it actually is that you want (a raise! an extra day of vacation! a new Aeron 'cause your back is fucking killing you!) exactly as you want it.

👊 Faith No More

Track your accomplishments so that you're relying on facts—not faith—when you ask for what you want. Even if you aren't ready to throw in the towel quite yet, keep a log so you have it when that blind faith runs out.

The Saboteur:
THE WOMENEMY

"There's a very special place in hell," Madeleine Albright has said, "for women who don't support other women." Of course, if that were true, many (most?) of us would be burning at the fiery gates.

Meet the Womenemy—also known as the Queen Bee, the Mean Girl, and the Unfriendly Firer. The Womenemy engages in sororicide, turning her weapons on her sisters in combat; viewing fellow fighters as enemies instead of allies.

---

so-ror-i-cide / n. The ultimate FFC war crime: Turning your weapon on your sisters in combat.

The Womenemy learns her place early, taught—from the moment she hits puberty—that she must compete with other women (for the attention of . . . men). Later, when that woman enters the workplace—which is, sadly, still likely to be run by men—she feels she must compete again to prove herself, elbowing aside the woman next to her in order to collect the golden ticket (or hold her place on the floor). It's easy to understand, in a way: if there are only few spots at the top, and only a few token women, then why wouldn't you view your sisters as the competition? Even women who try to help their fellow women can be penalized for it, facing more negative performance reviews than women who don't.

The Womenemy can take many forms:

THE GUYS' GAL, who believes that in order to succeed she must distance herself from, or undercut, the other women.

THE DOWN-ASS CHICK, who may go to extreme lengths to fit in with the guys, condoning their bad behavior—or acting as if it's hilarrrrrious—to prove she's on their level.

THE BASIC BROAD, who sees all women as the competition—assuming that one more woman in the room means *one less spot for her.*

THE GENERATIONAL GRENADE THROWER, or she who believes that because *she* had to suffer her way through the patriarchy of eras past, that you should too. (She may also take the form of the younger female colleague who thinks that female bosses are just "the worst.")

THE TAG-ALONG, or the woman who zombies her way through the working world, following along with group-think and perpetuating the stereotypes reflected by the masses.

It's easy to disdain these women—or to swear that we are nothing like them. And yet: 95 percent of working women have felt undercut by another woman at least once in their careers—which means most of us have either met her or *been* her.

THE FIGHT MOVES

👊 Vagffirmative Action

Remember rule No. 3 of the Feminist Fight Club: we fight *patriarchy*, not one another. Membership in the FFC means that you have taken an oath to help other women. And that doesn't just mean talking the talk—it means forwarding the résumé. Hire women. Promote women. Mentor women. *Do not* book a man for a panel, or a keynote, a meeting, a phone call, or any other kind of professional anything until you've booked an equal number of women. If you're hiring for an open position and the candidates are only men, insist on seeing an equal number of qualified women. The only way that we truly break down the tendency for women to compete against one another is to *get more of them in power*.

👊 Allies Not Enemies

Yup, even if you don't like her, show her that you're there for her like an underwire bra. If you find yourself in her bull's-eye, address conflict directly. Did you get off on the wrong foot? Invite her out for a drink. Tell her you want to be on the same team. Ask if you can clear the air. Make her your ally, not your enemy.

👊 When She Shines, You Shine

It's what besties Ann Friedman and Aminatou Sow, hosts of the podcast *Call Your Girlfriend*, call "Shine Theory"—the idea that another woman's success, or shine, is going to make you look brighter, not duller, by comparison. So instead of competing with awesome women or feeling jealous of their success, surround yourself with them—and bask in their glow.

👊 It's Not a Catfight

That whole Queen Bee syndrome? What if I told you it was bullshit? That, in fact, it's not that women are actually meaner to each other, it's that conflict among women is perceived differently than conflict among men (or even men and women)? When women have a conflict it's viewed as a "catfight"—irreparable and worthy of a grudge—but when men are involved it's simply a disagreement, something that happens at work, and can be moved on from.

👊 Clitoral Mass

Here's the truth: the more women in your office, the better off you are. Companies with more women on their boards have more female executives; more female CEOs or chairs means women in leadership—and better paid female leaders, at that. And the more female leaders there are, the more supported both junior and senior women feel. See? The problem isn't *other women*. It's a system that pits us against one another.

The Ten Commandments of Vagfirmative Action*

1. **Thou Shalt Support Other Women**
   Welcome and embrace them with bosom-like support.

2. **Thou Shalt Derive Strength from the Group**
   Once you begin to see all women as your sisters in combat, you will begin to feel invincible.

3. **Thou Shalt Employ a Strong Vagina-First* Policy**
   Hire women. Mentor women. Support women's ideas. You needn't be anti-penis, but you must consider a woman *first*.

4. **Thou Shalt Be Who the Fight Club Thinks You Are**
   Strong, confident, fierce. Let the cheers of your fellow fighters become the voice inside your head.

5. **Thou Shalt Vagfirm Each Other**
   Duties include: bragging on behalf of awesome ladies, publicly affirming a woman with a good idea, and lots of snaps.

6. **Thou Shalt Invest in Female Friendships**
   The only thing better than a self-confident woman is an army of them.

7. **Thou Shalt Ask for Help**
   Tap the power of the group. It is here to support you.

8. **Thou Shalt Respect Your Elders**
   We stand on the shoulder pads of the women who came before us.

9. **Thou Shalt Lift Up Your Juniors**
   Pass on your wisdom to the next generation. Help them rise up. Learn from them.

10. **Thou Shalt Help a Sister in Need**
    Once a month, you MUST do something to help another woman.

Also applicable to those who do not possess a vagina but identify as female

The Saboteur:
THE IMPOST-HER

"When a man, imagining his future career, looks in the mirror, he sees a senator staring back. A woman would never be so presumptuous."

—Marie Wilson, the creator of
Take Our Daughters to Work Day

Shortly after I was hired to be a columnist for *Time*'s website, I was asked to write about a book called *The Confidence Code.* Having actually been recruited and hired as a columnist, one would assume there'd be certain things I was capable of, *such as writing a column.* But this was my first column as a "columnist," and I was rattled. I labored over my introduction, writing and rewriting, deleting and retyping, cutting, pasting, moving sentences around, moving them around some more, then spending the next ten minutes Command-Z-ing my way back to where I'd started. Eventually, hunched over my sad desk (kitchen table) in my office (living room), clad in my freelancer's uniform (pajamas), I decided I had no business having a column at all. In fact, I was pretty sure my new contract would be revoked by the end of the week.

It wasn't—but the irony was that the book I was supposed to write about was about imposter syndrome, or that crippling sense of self-doubt that women often feel in the face of challenge, or *the very thing that was making it impossible for me to complete the task at hand.*

"Imposter syndrome" wasn't coined as a term until the 1970s, but it's safe to assume women have always felt it: that nagging feeling that, even after you've just done something *great,* maybe you actually don't deserve the praise. Imposter syndrome affects minority groups disproportionately: women, racial minorities, the LGBT population—or as Valerie Young, the author of a book on the topic, *The Secret Thoughts of Successful Women,* explains, people who have the pressure of "accomplishing firsts." It's common among high achievers, creative people, and students, and it persists in college, graduate school, and the working world.

Among the *types* of imposter syndrome:

• **Being absolutely 100 percent fucking sure you're going to fail.** Even Sheryl Sandberg, the unflappable COO of Facebook, has said she often feels this way. (Seriously, this woman is good at *everything.* This is absurd.) As she described it in her book, *Lean In:* "Every time I was called on in class, I was sure that I was about to embarrass myself. Every time I took a test, I was sure that it had gone badly. And every time I didn't embarrass myself—or even excelled—I believed that I had fooled everyone yet again. One day soon, the jig would be up."

• **Feeling like a complete fraud.** Or every so often, even when we've "made it," somehow being unable to shake the feeling that it's all smoke and mirrors, that we've still got everyone tricked, that at any moment we'll be found out and exposed. Three days before this manuscript was due to my editor, when I was alone in my apartment, running on no sleep, I remember walking into the bathroom and thinking to myself: *Why would anybody actually want to read about a bunch of experiences that are just . . . my own?* To which my editor, also a woman, later replied, "I constantly ask myself the same question about my editing."

• **Devaluing your worth—even as somebody else is actively supporting it.** In my case, that recently manifested as me talking somebody *out* of giving me money for work. "Why don't I just do it for free," I offered. To which a male friend—who happened to be in the room where this phone conversation was happening—practically shook me. "Jessica! Just take the money!" he said. (At which point I said yes.)

• **Underestimating your experience or expertise.** I was talking about this very thing with a friend who is a teacher, and in the next breath she told me about a job that she was being recruited for, followed by, "But I'm totally not qualified." (They had *recruited her*!) Another woman I interviewed—a postdoctoral engineering student named Celeste—told me that while she was working as a mechanical engineer, a supervisor once noted in her review that she wouldn't call herself an engineer. "I didn't realize I told my coworkers I wasn't an engineer when I was," Celeste said. "And I think, for me, it was an excuse just in case I made mistakes."

THE FIGHT MOVES

🤜 Find a Wingwoman

Talk to a colleague or friend: Has she felt like an imposter, too? Knowing this is a thing that others feel will help make it just that: a *thing*, but not *your* thing. If you feel that doubtful voice begin to creep inside your head, repeat: "It's not me, it's the imposter syndrome talking."

🤜 Squash Negative Self-Talk

Ask yourself what evidence exists that you are any *less* qualified than anybody else to do this work. Now ask what evidence exists that you are *just as qualified*—or even, I daresay, *more* qualified—to do the job. Make a list of at least ten things.

🤜 Failure Doesn't Make You a Fraud

When women screw up, they question their abilities or qualifications. (What did *I* do wrong?) But when men screw up, they point to bad luck, poor work, or not enough help from others—in other words, *outside forces*. Remember this: even the best athletes screw up, the best lawyers lose cases, the best actors star in busts. Don't let failure destroy your confidence.

🤜 Psyche Yourself Up

The words you say to yourself can actually change the way you *see* yourself—boosting confidence during a nerve-wracking event. So write yourself a Post-it or talk to yourself in the mirror. *Tell* yourself you are as fan-fucking-tastic as your male coworkers, and *forbid* yourself from falling back on excuses like luck to explain away your successes.

Visualize Success

Olympic athletes do it; so do military officers. Visualize precisely how you'll navigate the situation—successfully—before it happens.

Overprepare

For the task at hand—just to preempt any potential feeling of fraudulence or insecurity. German chancellor Angela Merkel has said she does this to overcome her doubts. Managing director of the IMF Christine Lagarde acknowledges that she overprepares regularly. As Lagarde has explained it, "When we work on a particular matter, we will work the file inside, outside, sideways, backwards, historically, genetically, and geographically. We want to be completely on top of everything and we want to understand it all and we don't want to be fooled by somebody else."

Unsubscribe from Doubt

In his book, *Originals*, the scholar Adam Grant describes two kinds of doubt: *self*-doubt—which causes you to freeze up—and *idea* doubt, which can actually motivate people to work on refining, testing, or experimenting with a good idea. Try to turn self-doubt into idea doubt by telling yourself, it's not that I'm crap, it's that the first few drafts of *any* idea are always crap—and I'm just not there yet.

FAMOUS IMPOST-HERS

TINA FEY

"The beauty of the impostor syndrome is you vacillate between extreme egomania, and a complete feeling of: 'I'm a fraud! Oh god, they're on to me! I'm a fraud!'"

FRAUD

SONIA SOTOMAYOR

The Supreme Court justice has said that at Princeton, she felt like she was waiting for someone to tap her on the shoulder and say, "You don't belong!"

DOESN'T BELONG

MAYA ANGELOU

Yes, her. The prizewinning author once said, after her eleventh book, that every time she wrote another one she'd think to herself, "Uh oh, they're going to find out now. I've run a game on everybody."

EXPOSED

KIRSTEN GILLIBRAND

The senator didn't have the confidence to run for office until she volunteered for other people's campaigns for ten years. What held her back? "Am I good enough? Am I tough enough? Am I strong enough? Am I smart enough? Am I qualified?"

UNQUALIFIED

JODIE FOSTER

The actress has said she thought it was a fluke she got into Yale—and that she won an Academy Award. "I thought everybody would find out, and they'd take the Oscar back. They'd come to my house, knocking on the door, 'Excuse me, we meant to give that to someone else. That was going to Meryl Streep.'"

A MISTAKE

MERYL STREEP

When asked in an interview if she would always act, the woman with the most Oscars in history replied, "You think, 'Why would anyone want to see me again in a movie?' I don't know how to act anyway, so why am I doing this?"

AMATEUR

MICHELLE OBAMA

As a young woman, the lawyer and first lady used to lie awake at night asking herself, "Am I too loud? Too much? Dreaming too big?" "Eventually, I just got tired of always worrying what everyone else thought of me. So I decided not to listen."

NOT GOOD ENOUGH

The Saboteur:
THE HERFECTIONIST

At Stanford, they call it "duck syndrome:" there you are, appearing to glide seamlessly above water, all the while underneath the surface you're paddling frantically to stay afloat. At Penn State, it goes by "Penn face," to describe those who master the art of appearing to be happy and self-assured, even when they're struggling or stressed out. At Duke, the phenomenon has been called "effortless perfection"—or the pressure felt by college women to be "smart, accomplished, fit, beautiful and popular," all without any "visible effort."

The seeds of the Herfectionist may be planted in adolescence and sprout in college, but they continue to grow well into our adult lives, where women's mistakes are noticed more and remembered longer (and judged even more harshly if she's a woman of color). The Herfectionist places immense, almost unbearable pressure on herself, setting astronomically high—almost unattainable—goals, without even considering the possibility of a setback (failure is not an option). But when the bar for achievement is so high, so unrealistic, paralyzing self-criticism is inevitable. And so, at the first sign of a speed bump, the Herfectionist often gives up. That is, if she doesn't find herself headed for a nervous breakdown first.

THE FIGHT MOVES

👊 Take a Victory Lap

While self-criticism comes easily to the Herfectionist, rarely does she take the time to celebrate her *victories*. So pop a cork every now and then and give yourself a pat on the back—and be aware of even the small accomplishments that inch you closer to your goal.

👊 Baby Steps

This doesn't mean lowering your standards, but setting *incremental* targets—and making sure they're specific—so you know when you've reached them. Think of it like building a Lego tower. Each time you achieve a small goal, you're locking in another piece. And if your tenth block falls down, the rest of the tower will remain standing.

👊 Ask For Help

You don't have to "do it all"—asking for help makes you look *more* competent, not less. Give yourself permission to do it.

👊 Know When to Fold 'Em

It's been shown that grit—or sticking with a long-term goal to its completion—can be a gateway to success. But the *refusal* to give up on unreachable goals can also cause a huge amount of stress. Ambition is great, but there are also times you have to recognize when a goal just isn't realistic. Try to notice how much pressure you're putting on yourself—and whether it's time to try something different.

The Saboteur:
THE NERVOUS RAMBLER

Call it a slow train wreck of the mouth. The Nervous Rambler is not necessarily a *talker*. She doesn't ramble in normal conversation. But when she's on the spot—a presentation, a negotiation, or anything where the stakes are high—her nerves get the best of her and she simply *can't. stop. talking.* She speaks fast, adds extra words, trails off, then repeats herself until her message is lost in the jumble. We've all been in a situation where we walk out of a high-tension situation and wonder what the hell we just said—but The Nervous Rambler speaks like the mic is about to be physically yanked out of her hand.

THE FIGHT MOVES

✊ 140 Characters or Less

OK not actually—but when answering a question or pitching an idea, try to contain your response to a single, conclusive Tweet (or maybe two). Give yourself a word or phrase that signals when you need to wrap it up. Whatever limit you choose to set, the point is to force yourself to be succinct and *then stop talking*. If you're asked follow-up questions, sure, keep going. If you aren't: STFU.

✊ Track Your TMIs

If, in the aftermath of an interview or important presentation, you regret having rambled, make note and try to figure out what compelled it. Catch yourself before you do it next time.

✊ Deep Breaths

People tend to speak faster when they're nervous. Deep breaths tell your sympathetic nervous system—the network of nerves that controls our fight-or-flight response—to chill out, and your cortisol (the stress hormone) to take a break.

✊ Silence Is Your BFF

Nobody likes an awkward silence, but it can also be your most powerful tool. Remember this about a long pause: it gives you time to breathe. It lets the impact of your words hang in the air. It can force the other person to speak first. So try to embrace the silence when the time is right—and let the other party be the one to start rambling.

The Saboteur:
THE BURNOUT

The Burnout exists in a world in which superhuman-like stamina is often required of women, and yet very few of us (if any) actually possess it. Men burn out too, but not as much: in one study of eighteen- to forty-four-year-olds, women were almost twice as likely as men to say they felt "very tired," "exhausted," or worn out most days. That, and overworking negatively affects women's health more than men's. And for women with children? When the first shift ends, the second one begins: kids, laundry, dinner, homework—all things that still disproportionately fall on women's shoulders. Wouldn't you burn out?

THE FIGHT MOVES

👊 Cell-Free Zone

"Work will happen twenty-four hours a day, 365 days a year if you let it," the Hollywood showrunner Shonda Rhimes has said. So set boundaries: when you'll leave the office, the time you stop checking email. If you have the ability to do so, state these limits publicly so they set a precedent for others. Here's what Rhimes's email signature states:

> *Please Note*: I will not engage in work emails after 7 pm or on weekends. *IF I AM YOUR BOSS, MAY I SUGGEST: PUT DOWN YOUR PHONE.*

👊 Get Down with OTP (Overtime Prevention)

Many people put in late hours as a way to show their commitment— and hope it pays off in the long run. But all that overtime doesn't necessarily pay off for women, in part because they likely bear the brunt of the work at home, too: as one study found, in workplaces that place top value on "overwork," women are in fact more likely to be evaluated poorly and less likely to receive opportunities for promotions.

👊 Max 'n' Relax

The biggest difference between men's and women's time at home is that men get more *leisure* time than women—five hours more each week, according to Pew. The less time you give yourself to recuperate, to chill, to just *relax,* the greater your burnout risk. So: Add time to your calendar. Or, better yet: clear everything from it, and slowly add the important things back in. Stop feeling guilty for going for a walk on your lunch break. Make time for *you*—and the things that will help you keep your stress levels in check.

👊 Ruthless Prioritization

Enough with the *shoulda coulda woulda.* If you feel you're headed for burnout, be ruthless about what you say yes to. Try the following: say no to everything that does not provide something crucial in return—so no more "shoulds," only "musts" and "wants" (and sometimes even "wants" need to be cut back). That means the choir you joined, the office sports league you got pressured into showing up for, or the extra shift you agreed to take for a coworker who's going out of town—nope! When you're *not* on the verge of burnout, you can come back to these things. But for now, "shoulds" are simply not up for discussion.

GET YO' NAP IN, GURL!

In her book *Thrive,* Arianna Huffington describes a Harvard study that found lack of sleep to be a "significant factor" in the Exxon *Valdez* wreck, the explosion of the Space Shuttle *Challenger,* and the nuclear accidents at Chernobyl and Three Mile Island. Getting enough sleep is especially important for women: at least one study has found that women suffer more than men—both mentally and physically—when they don't get adequate sleep, and that they generally need more sleep than men, too (hey, a lady's gotta work twice as hard, right?). So try this bit of FFC-approved advice: don't skimp on sleep! When in doubt— or feeling lazy, guilty, or like you've got too much to do—remember: Winston Churchill, John F. Kennedy, and Leonardo da Vinci rank among history's most famous nappers. Womanpropriate *that*.

Part Three

BOOBY TRAPS

OFFICE STEREOTYPES and HOW to HACK 'EM

OK, so it *sounded* glamorous: Smita had just returned from a month on the road in Europe, filming a pilot for a television series she'd scripted across thirteen cities. But Vespa-ing around the Mediterranean with a camera, sipping Pellegrino at sunset in Paris she was not. After months of pitching, casting, and rewriting her script, landing a small sum from a New York production company to film the pilot, quitting her day job and borrowing money so she could do it, she was working fourteen-hour days overseas, crammed into cheap hotel rooms with her crew to stretch their budget and gunning to hit seven countries in four weeks. Even under the best of circumstances, it would have been a grueling schedule.

And these were not exactly the best of circumstances. Despite being a seasoned producer—she'd worked on a half-dozen TV sets, managed sprawling professional crews, and assisted high-profile filmmakers—this was Smita's first time directing on her own. She was assigned a crew of eight men: two with drinking problems, three with Adderall habits, all eight extraordinarily difficult to manage (and not just because they couldn't seem to *once* show up on time).

It was not exactly the trip of a lifetime. Smita was on the verge of a nervous breakdown.

And so she tried every tactic she could think of to get the crew in line. She asked for their feedback on the script, to try to get them invested in it—and dutifully tried out their suggestions, even when she knew they wouldn't work. She tried to be accommodating—asking what she could do to make their jobs easier, bringing them coffee in the morning to try to get them out of bed. "I realized that wasn't working," she later said, drolly, "because they kept handing me their notebooks and their jackets to hold and asking me to get them things out of the van."

She tacked again, trying to play it cool. When they'd opt to do it *their* way—on *her* set—she'd try to be enthusiastic in her initial responses: "Awesome!" she'd trill, "but let's try it this way first!" They tuned her out. Next she went for the plaintive thing, appealing to their guilt—"Hey guys-s-s-s, can we *please* try to be on time to set tomorrow?" But it made her feel like a nag.

Finally, she cut the crap and pulled rank. She demanded they show up on time. "How about we do it this way?" was replaced by "I don't have time for this. *Follow the fucking script.*"

It worked . . . sorta. They obeyed, albeit with disdain. When the set closed for the day, they'd head off to the bar to escape her. Everyone was grouchy. She was getting the show she'd wanted, finally—but her team was hardly speaking to her (or each other).

Then one day, in their last country, Germany, in their very last week of filming, a local cameraman came to set with a case of dried meat sticks—apparently some kind of regional specialty. He set them down, and Smita turned to her lead. "You can have one if you say your lines the way I asked!" she joked, dangling an oversized piece of jerky in his face.

To her surprise, he did it. And suddenly, the other guys on set wanted to know: Could they have meat sticks too?

It was as if she'd cracked a secret code.

"Being one of the guys didn't work. Trying to have conversations about girls didn't work. Mothering them didn't work. Nothing worked," Smita recalled, sitting in my living room during an afternoon bitch session. "I tried to look prettier, I tried to look less pretty. I pretended for a day that I was not a vegetarian because I thought maybe *that* was why they weren't relating to me. But in the end, it was meat sticks. The meat sticks worked."

The reductive view of this parable is, of course, that dudes can be trained like golden retrievers, behaving only by the grace of a showily wielded treat. And that may be true . . . to an extent (unless of course the men in your office are vegan).

But really, the meat is not the point. The point is that being a boss of any kind is hard, but being a boss *as a woman* is like an obstacle course—a maze of stereotypes, land mines, and invisible booby traps surprising you at every turn. Oh, she asked you twice for something? What a *nag*. She made a demand? She's such a *diva*. She raised her voice? Must be 'cause she's out-of-control *angry*.

And then there are the challenges of simply trying to find a leadership style that works: not too authoritative, or you'll be deemed unfeminine, but not too feminine, either—go too girly and you're suddenly emotional, soft, not capable of making the tough calls, the babysitter asked to hold your underlings' coats.

And on and on and on . . .

If women had known to speak softly and carry a big meat stick, perhaps the revolution might already have been won. But in the meantime—or at least until those German meat sticks make their way to America—the best thing we can do is sharpen our eyes to spot the traps, the stereotypes, and the hidden biases we are statistically almost guaranteed to face. And maybe have a backup meat-stick plan.

The Trap:
"FEMALE BOSSES ARE THE WORST"

You may think she fits the stereotype of the ice-cold female boss, but you are likely the colleague, or underling, who is actually more critical (and demanding) of her because she's female*— expecting her to fill the role of boss, mommy, and best friend at once, running the show with both authority *and* grace while being warm, nurturing, and supportive (and look good while she's doing it). It is not *un*true that some female bosses may be harder on women because they're women—but it is most certainly true, statistically, that their employees are harder on them because they're women, too.

---

* Yup, research confirms that female employees hold their female managers to different standards than they do their male managers.

THE HACK

🥊 Femlightenment

So yes, Americans may think they prefer male bosses—by an average of 33 percent, no matter their gender or education level, according to recent studies. (Ooof.) But if you dig deeper into that data you'll find a revealing caveat: that the majority of people who say they prefer having a male boss have never actually had a female boss. Those who had worked for a woman before in fact preferred reporting to women. So help your fellow woman out and give her the benefit of the doubt—and remind your colleagues to do the same.

TOO AMBITIOUS

HILLARY CLINTON
PRESIDENTIAL CANDIDATE

A BULLY ON THE BENCH

DIFFICULT

BLUNT

SONIA SOTOMAJOR
SUPREME COURT
JUSTICE

UPPITY
BITCH

CONDOLEEZZA RICE,
FORMER SECRETARY OF
STATE

STUBBORN
BOSSY

RUTH BADER GINSBERG,
SUPREME COURT JUSTICE

The Trap:
"BITCHY, BOSSY, TOO AMBITIOUS"

In early 2016, if you were to google "Bernie Sanders" and "ambition," you would have found a host of articles about his "ambitious plans," think pieces about "ambitious health-care goals," and assorted other posts commending his professional determination. But the same web search for Hillary Clinton would yield just the opposite. Of more than 1 million results, the top hits would focus on her "lifelong" *personal* ambition: "unbridled," "ruthless," even "pathological." In a word: unappealing.

Behold the catch-22 of women and power. To be successful a woman must be liked, but to be liked she must not be too successful: her likability eroded by her professional status. We may all know—or at least like to say we know—that women are perfectly capable as leaders. Yet on a deep, unconscious level we still find the image of an ambitious woman hard to swallow. The reasoning makes sense: for hundreds of years, it's been culturally ingrained in us that men lead and women nurture. So when a woman turns around and exhibits "male" traits—ambition, assertion, sometimes even aggression—we somehow see her as too masculine, not ladylike enough, and thus we like her less.

THE HACKS

🤛 Get Your Sexism in Check

All of us—yes, really, all of us—are a little bit sexist (racist, too). It's what scholars call "unconscious bias," and each of us has it; the result of cognitive shortcuts made by our brains. The good news is that if we acknowledge our inner sexist we can check it. So the next time an ambitious woman rubs you the wrong way, ask yourself: Would I dislike her if she were a man?

🤛 Gender Judo

As research by the Harvard professor Amy Cuddy has shown, "warmth" has been shown to help offset the trap of being "too ambitious," because it counters the stereotype that ambitious women are cold, power-hungry bitches. We shouldn't have to do it, no, but it's what the law professor Joan C. Williams has called "gender judo"—or combining communal behaviors like friendliness, humor, empathy, or kindness (the sugar) with aggression or ambition. Studies show it works. If you think about it, most of the world's best leaders have mastered this art: they may be tough, but they're known for their grace and humor, too.

🤛 Make Female Power the Norm

As the economist Sylvia Ann Hewlett once told me, it's not *women* who are the problem—it's that we still define leadership in male terms. So use that sweetness, that ambition, or the combination of the two, to *get the fuck in power*. Make ambition a *female* trait. Chip away at that glass ceiling and don't apologize for it. And when you've trailblazed your way to the top, remember your FFC duty: to bring other women with you.

The Trap:
"SHE'S TOO *NICE* TO LEAD THE TEAM"

Ebonee was everything a political campaign might want in an intern. She was smart: sailing through college in three years and graduating at the top of her class. She was committed: volunteering to stay late and helping others finish their work. She was unwavering: when voters would stop by the office, she knew them by name. Yet when it was announced that the campaign would hire from its intern pool for a staff position, Ebonee didn't get the job. As the campaign manager put it: "Ebonee is too nice. She can't be taken seriously."

Being nice *shouldn't* undermine the perception of a person's competence, yet when it comes to women we tend to view the two traits as inversely related—a surplus of one leading to the belief you're deficient in the other. So when a woman is nice, or even just *described* as nice, we assume she's dumb, ditzy, or a pushover—when in fact we have no information about her skills at all.

THE HACK

✊ Sweet like Arsenic

Use niceness to your advantage—by mastering the art of being nice and tough at once. Cloak your demands in sweetness, but make the demand. Become a master of giving orders or asking for what you need in a pleasant tone. Don't become the office shoulder to cry on and don't become the Office Mom (see page 55). But it is possible to play nice while still being taken seriously.

✊ Watch Your Words

Cut the word "nice" from your vocabulary—along with all those other nurturing words we use to describe women ("kind," "helpful," "a team player"). Not only are women only more likely to be described by such language, but research has found that those words cause them to be viewed as less qualified—perceived as pushovers, not somebody capable of running a team. So next time you have the urge to describe your female colleague as "sympathetic," try one of these "male" words instead: independent, confident, intelligent, fair.

REPEAT AFTER ME:
Just because I'm <u>NICE</u>
Don't assume I'm a
PUSHOVER
(NOW WRITE THAT DOWN AND TACK
IT TO YOUR CUBICLE WALL)

The Trap:
"YOU DON'T *LOOK* LIKE AN ENGINEER"

It didn't take long for twenty-two-year-old software engineer Isis Anchalee Wenger to feel the wrath of the Internet. In 2015, the San Franciscan woman was asked to appear in a recruiting ad for her company. "My team is great, everyone is smart, great, and hilarious," the advertisement read, along with her photo, appearing on buses throughout her city. There was just one problem: commuters—or at least those who chose to make her likeness go viral—thought Wenger was too pretty to be a "real" engineer. Or perhaps she was just too female. Because while much ink has been spilled to the fact that pretty people of both genders earn more money than average-looking people, a woman can't change the fact that she most likely looks like . . . a woman. As long as men dominate certain industries, "female" will not be the norm.

THE HACK

🫱 Twirl on Them Haters

Justin Trudeau is "pretty"—does anyone think that makes him a worse politician? Some might say Mark Zuckerberg is not—and he's worth $35 billion. Do you think either of these men has to answer questions about his competence because of the way he looks? Wenger started a hashtag, #ILookLikeAnEngineer, and hundreds of female engineers submitted photos of themselves holding up signs that read: "This is what an engineer looks like." Guess what? They *all looked different*. If somebody thinks you don't look like a [fill in the blank], ignore them—and just keep talking. Eventually they'll have to hear the words coming out of your mouth rather than judging you by your appearance.

9 TO FLY:
A HERSTORY OF OFFICE DRESS

Colored pencils not included.

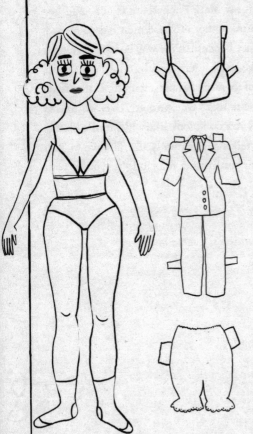

Bra

In the 1970s, the underwear company Bali introduced a "soft bra" whose slogan read: "How to wear a bra and look like you're not." It was, as one bra executive put it, a kind of "bosom consciousness."

Boxy Suit

Shoulder pads and the floppy tie became iconic symbols of '80s boxy suit androgyny, designed to mask a woman's shape so it wouldn't hinder her ability to move up the corporate ladder.

Bloomers

Named for Amelia Bloomer, a postmistress and suffragette, the bloomer allowed women to move freely—casting off the heavy skirts and starched petticoats.

Culottes

They look like skirts, they hang like skirts, but they're actually . . . pants! Culottes emerged in the early 1900s in response to the era's bicycle craze. (*You* try riding a bike in a 20-pound hoop skirt.)

Pants

It wasn't until 1973 that secretaries in our very own White House were allowed to wear pants—when the energy crisis led to lowered thermostats and chillier working conditions.

Miniskirt

The designer Mary Quant is credited as the mini-skirt's pioneer, famously remarking that 1960s style should be "arrogant, aggressive, and sexy."

Maxiskirt

The calf-length maxiskirt was a favorite among 1950s suburbanites who loved it for al fresco dining, but when it reemerged as office-wear in the 1960s there was pandemonium: men complained it would spoil the pleasure of looking at miniskirted legs; a cosmetics executive threatened to fire a long-skirted employee; and a Southern politician announced he'd kick any woman in a maxiskirt out of the state house.

High Heels

Originally worn by men (the European aristocracy, among others, as a signal of status), women adopted the heel in the early 1600s as a way to appropriate power (smart ladies!).

The Trap:
"WHAT A NAG!"

One of the crowning political achievements of the women's movement was the passage of the Nineteenth Amendment, in 1920, which granted women the right to vote. Yet even back then, the (female) president of a group opposed to suffrage noted that allowing women to cast their vote would "be an official endorsement of *nagging* as a national policy." It's funny to think about—except that even a hundred years later, the stereotype of the nagging woman persists—and not just in the home. A man asks for something twice at work? Wow, he must really need it. But how many times have you heard a woman called a nag for the same behavior?

THE HACKS

🗣 Find a Nag Hag

Enlist a friend to contribute to the nagging. By getting *them* to follow up on the small stuff—and have the check-ins come from different angles—it ensures you don't come off as the "naggy" one.

🗣 Multimedia Nagger

Switch up the *way* you check in. You already sent two emails, OK— pick up the phone and call this person. If they don't answer, walk by their desk. It's harder to ignore you if you get up in their face.

🗣 Every Day I'm Nudgin'

Just remember: you can't get fired for nudging people (especially if it's *your job* to nudge people). So if shit needs doing, and the person who should be doing it isn't, communicate deadlines, indicate there are consequences for missing them, and then, demand that they get done. If you're not in a position to make demands, and you feel timid about reaching out again, employ the mantra we'll discuss in part six: WWJD: What Would Josh Do?

The Trap:
"PSYCHO ALERT!"

SPEAKS LOUD
NOT SMILING
HAS OPINIONS
DIAGNOSIS:
HYSTERIA

"Hysteria" was once a catchall medical diagnosis for a woman with "problems"—used to explain away anything from anxiety to insomnia to lack of sexual desire.* Yet the trope of the "crazy," "emotional," "moody," ""hysterical" psycho-woman remains: a blanket put-down for that ex-girlfriend who stopped calling you, the woman who dared make a demand at work, or anyone in Hollywood who—as Tina Fey has put it—"keeps talking, even after no one wants to f*ck her anymore." There is no conclusive evidence to support that women are *actually* more emotional at work. But there is research to support that female emotion is *perceived* differently than men's.

---

* In some cases solved by male doctors manually stimulating the women with a rudimentary vibrator. Ah, "science"!

THE HACKS

Say What?

I'd say take a deep breath and try to calm down, but that's the whole point: this happens when women *are perfectly calm*. So next time a colleague insinuates that a woman is "crazy," play dumb. Say, "I'm not sure I understand. Can you explain?" and put the burden on *them* to stumble through the explanation.

Diagnosis: Passion

Research shows that when a woman expresses emotion at work, people assume she's being "hormonal," while men are simply viewed as "passionate" about the job. If you *are* emotional—not like "I'm on my period/crying in the office" emotional, but expressing legitimate feeling about something work-related emotional—try explaining the *reason* for that emotion (literally: "I'm emotional because you fucked up this project"). It makes the emotion about the *work*, not you.

The Trap:
"WHY ARE YOU SO ANGRY?"

The stereotype of the Angry Black Woman is a reliable trope: hostile, loud, self-sufficient to a fault. It exists in pop culture, in our offices, and even in public life: Remember that group of African American women who were kicked off a Napa Valley wine train for being too "loud"? Or what about that *New York Times* profile of Shonda Rhimes, in which the writer wondered whether a TV titan lauded for her strong black female characters might title her autobiography, *How to Get Away with Being an Angry Black Woman*?

The threat of this stereotype is multifold: if they're already perceived as "angry"—and research shows they are*—then black women may also be more likely to fall victim to the "too aggressive" trap, penalized for the same behavior that gets rewarded in men. It also creates a constant sense of having to modify one's behavior. As the writer Huda Hassan explained it in an article for BuzzFeed, "As a black woman in public, I'm hyperconscious of my actions, tone, and words out of fear that I might seem too angry."

---

* In one study, conducted by the psychologist Roxanne Donovan, white undergraduates were asked to describe typical black and typical white women from among a list of provided adjectives. Let's just say that "loud," "talkative," and "tough" only applied to one group.

THE HACKS

🤜 Keep It on the Record

In Rhimes's case, many called for the *Times* article to be retracted, but she preferred to keep it on the record—as a kind of historical document. "In this world in which we all feel we're so full of gender equality and we're a postracial [society] . . . it's a very good reminder to see the casual racial bias and odd misogyny from a woman written in a paper that we all think of as being so liberal," she said.

🤜 Have a Good Retort

Call it the Amandla Stenberg approach: When the teen actress was called "too angry" on Twitter she responded with the following: "I have strong opinions. I am not angry." What she perhaps unknowingly employed was a trick advised by the law professor Joan C. Williams in her book *What Works for Women at Work*: that to offset the stereotype of the out-of-control angry woman, it can work to reframe the emotion as something other than anger (or justify it based on cause). Stenberg reframed it as being opinionated; in an office setting, Williams has advised tying any emotion back to a shared business goal. So if he says, "I don't know why you're so *upset*," you say, "I'm not *upset*. I'm *concerned* about our progress."

Don't Get Mad, Get Even

Which means having an *even* number of women of color in your office in proportion to the population. Whether that means passing along a résumé, making an effort to offer support to young women of color, this task shouldn't fall only to the minorities in the room. The more diverse your office, the better off it will be—and suddenly, being "mad" will be seen for what it really is: not actually "mad" at all.

The Trap:
"WHY DON'T YOU SMILE?"

Call this a brief history of dudes asking ladies to *smile real purty*: Hillary Clinton, after a significant primary win. ("Smile," tweeted the MSNBC host Joe Scarborough, "you just had a big night."); Serena Williams, after a grueling match at the U.S. Open. (Reporter: "You just won a match. Normally you smile when you win . . . What's wrong?"); and probably, at one point or another, *you*. Newsflash: women are not actually *required* to smile every minute of the day (nor are we always that happy). Yet there's a persistent sense that if we aren't, something must be terribly wrong. (Is she angry? Upset? PMSing? Or does she simply suffer from Resting Bitch Face?)

THE HACK

The Broad City Approach:

HIM: Smile!

YOU: [Places a middle fingers at each corner of mouth. Curls upward.]

WANTED
UNSMILING WOMAN

W2481

UNSMILING WOMAN
AGE: 28
HEIGHT: 5'5
EYE COLOR: BROWN
EXPRESSION: BITCHY

LAST SEEN: STARING DOWN MALE
COWORKER
CRIME: RESTING BITCH FACE

IF YOU HAVE ANY INFORMATION
LEADING TO THIS SUSPECT
PLEASE CONTACT HR
IMMEDIATELY

The Trap:
"THERE WEREN'T ANY QUALIFIED CANDIDATES"

You've heard me say it by now: To be a woman in the working world means to have to work twice as hard and be twice as good, simply to be viewed on par with a man at her same level. But to be a woman of color is to endure a double threat: the burden of both gender and race, where the odds are triply, quadruply, quintuply stacked against her. Studies show that black, Hispanic, and Asian women are actually *more* ambitious than their white counterparts—and yet they consistently report feeling stalled. And how could they not? The barriers begin before they've even gotten *in the door,* where job applicants with a "black-sounding name" had to have *eight additional years of experience* in order to get the same number of callbacks as someone with an identical résumé but a white-sounding name.

THE HACK

👊 Look Harder

For bosses: don't just sit around talking about diversity—recruit for it. Or, better yet, create a blind application process. The comedian Samantha Bee used one for her late-night show, and the result was a launch staff that was half female and 30 percent nonwhite (as well as a brilliant show). J. J. Abrams, the director of the newest *Star Wars,* has a policy at his production company that requires any list of writers, directors, actors, or producers to be representative of the gender and racial makeup in America—which breaks down to roughly 50 percent women, 12 percent black, 18 percent Hispanic, and 6 percent Asian. "No qualified candidates" is no longer an excuse.

The Trap:
"LONE WOMAN IN THE ROOM"

"People ask me sometimes, When—when do you think it will be enough? When will there be enough women on the court? And my answer is when there are nine."

—Supreme Court justice Ruth Bader Ginsburg

Former White House deputy chiefs of staff Nancy-Ann DeParle and Alyssa Mastromonaco called it "Smurfette syndrome": while working in the Obama White House, they joked that they were the administration's "Smurfettes," the lone female character on the animated show, created by mistake, in a village of male Smurfs. But the reality of being those lone female Smurfs—even if you're not literally alone—is significant, because research shows that it requires a certain number of women to have an impact on a majority-male room. Without it? Women speak up less, they have less influence, and people tend to think that because they're speaking *as* a woman that they're speaking on behalf of *all* women. No pressure, right?

THE HACK

🤛 Support Your Local Girl Gang

Meaning the one in your office. Look around the room. How many women are present? The goal is to reach *at the very least* a third. That's the point of "critical mass," as psychology studies have put it, at which a woman's perspective is more likely to be heard and her opinions less likely to be perceived as representing her entire *gender* (or her gender *and* her race) rather than herself. Remember: white men constitute just 31 percent of the American population. There is no situation in which they should be constituting the majority of the room. So whether it's informing your bosses, passing along another woman's résumé, or anonymously tacking a list of reasons why an equally balanced office is actually *better* (see page xxvi)—do what you can to send a message to your employers that they must do better.

The Trap:
"HOW DO I FIND A MENTOR?"

"You don't have to have mentors who look like you.
Had I been waiting for a black, female Soviet spe-
cialist mentor, I would still be waiting."

—Condoleezza Rice

Having somebody to advise you on your career is important for everyone—but for women it's often crucial, because they're coming from a disadvantage. Yet there's a supply problem when it comes to such advisors for women, and not just because two-thirds of male executives are hesitant to have one-on-one meetings with junior women (because it might be taken the wrong way). Women tend to rely on other women for mentors, which is excellent—except that most of us still work in places where it's mostly men in charge.

THE HACK

PBOD (Personal Board of Directors)

"Mentor" may be the business world's favorite buzzword of the moment, but people don't just *emerge* into the working world with mentors—those relationships develop over time. So what can you do if you're just starting out? Here's one idea: create a group of mentors. One friend has one she calls her PBOD—or "personal board of directors"—who weigh in on one another's decisions and dilemmas. A PBOD (*or a Fight Club for that matter*) doesn't require you to find one specific person to "be your mentor"—and it's a less weighty ask: you're spreading the advice around (and giving some back, too).

WOMAN SEEKS PBOD
FOR MENTORSHIP, CASUAL ADVICE

EQUAL OPPORTUNIST
Seeking diversity by race, sexual orientation, and gender. No age preference.

NOT LOOKING FOR FRIENDS
Must be able to give no-bullshit advice on a range of professional topics.

NON-EXCLUSIVITY
Please know you're not the only one in my PBOD.

DEFINING THE RELATIONSHIP
I won't ask you to wear my promise ring, but I would like to know it's OK to go to you for advice on a semi-regular basis.

NO GHOSTING
Staying in touch is important.

RELATIONSHIP RECIPROCITY
I'd like to repay the favor—by being there for you if you ever need it. What sets apart a PBOD from a mentor is that you are often advising *each other*.

NO DICK PICS
Let's keep it classy, 'k?

The Trap:
"SHE'S SUCH A GOSSIP"

Sure, sometimes women gather around the coffee machine or huddle in a break room. There are occasions, yes, when they may be chatting about something other than work. This isn't a bad thing—socializing is essential for your career. Yet it's women, not men, who get docked for being "too chatty" at work,* the sight of them talking somehow connoting less "serious" conversation (or the verge of a catfight). In an office setting, even such benign behavior as frequent phone calls—or gathering around the water cooler—is more likely to be called "gossip" when it's done by women.

THE HACK

---

* Ironic since it's actually *men* who speak up more.

The Trap:
"AM I CONFIRMING THE STEREOTYPE?"

So you get hired at a company that likes to tout its commitment to "diversity," yet you are one of just a few women on the team. Day after day, you're in rooms dominated by white men, passing them in the hallways, being asked to help them out on projects, and suddenly you start to wonder if they're looking at you funny, scrutinizing you because you're the only *other* in the room. One day one of them questions your work. Another asks, either innocently or not, "Where are you *from*?" The pressure builds up and you start to second-guess yourself. You're angry, you're irritated, but you're also anxious: *You simply cannot fuck this up or you will prove the stereotype right.* You must be *bulletproof.* Then you make a small mistake and suddenly you begin to spiral. It's like institutional Stockholm syndrome, but worse: a combination of imposter syndrome (that phenomenon where high-achieving women and minorities feel like they don't belong); stereotype threat (the fear that you will confirm the worst stereotypes about yourself—performing worse as a result); as well as *actual* sexism and racism thrown in (yes, often women and minorities really *are* held to a higher standard—their mistakes noticed more and remembered longer).

THE HACKS

🥊 Verbal Karate

Arm yourself with facts. Diverse teams are more profitable, more productive, and more collaborative. This is not speculation, it is science: your very *presence* is strengthening the team at large.

🥊 Believe Your Own Hype

Particularly if you're not getting the outside affirmation you deserve. Writing affirmations is one way to do this—shown to boost confidence and improve performance. Writing down your successes is another method—so you can look back on them every time you feel a hint of self-doubt coming on. It is essential to remind yourself of the amazing shit you've done to squash that negative self-talk (or, as my friend Tanya Tarr, a career coach, puts it: "That negative voice doesn't pay your rent, so bounce that freeloading fucker out").

Insp-her-ation

Keep a picture (or five) of a female role model, particularly if she shares your background. No, you don't have to creepily pull a crumpled photo out of your purse—just screenshot something on your phone. Look at it before you head into a big meeting or right before any anxiety-inducing event: this simple trick can help women speak publicly and perform more confidently.

Underest-him-ation

Use any underestimation of your talent to your gain. Slay the assignment, win the negotiation, run intellectual circles around your opponent while they sit there trying to catch their breath. Let their underestimation become your WMD. And then swivel around in your chair and say, ever so politely, "Boom." (Also, keep a record of all the assignments you've slayed, so that when your boss expresses hesitation on your readiness for a promotion, you can attach it in an email to him. Subject line: Bitches Get Sh*t Done.)

The Trap:
"SHE'S TOO OLD"

"I have so many questions about getting older as a woman," the comedian Jena Friedman joked onstage. "Like, how will I be able to hail cabs once I become . . . *invisible*?" The Invisible Woman logic goes like this: We live in a world where women are still viewed as sex objects; where being beautiful reaps workplace benefits (for women and men); and where *youth* appears to be the baseline requirement for beauty (why else would we spend so much money on Botox?). Age bias affects both genders—but it affects women more. (You know how men with gray hair are still considered "distinguished," while women are just old?) It's why male actors peak at forty-six, while female actors tap out at thirty and it's why even hiring managers say openly that a "qualified but visibly older" candidate would make them hesitate (particularly if that candidate was female). All of which leaves women, as the Stanford law professor Deborah Rhode once put it, "not only perpetually worried about their appearance but also worried about worrying."

ACT MY AGE?
WHAT **THE FUCK** IS THAT,

'ACT MY AGE'

WHAT DO I CARE HOW
OLD I AM?

THE OCEAN IS OLD AS FUCK

IT WILL STILL DROWN YOUR ASS WITH VIGOR

THE HACK

👊 **Fucks Given: Zero**

Your assignment, class? The Amy Schumer sketch, "Last Fuckable Day," in which Tina Fey, Julia Louis-Dreyfus, and Patricia Arquette hold a funeral for Julia's vagina (and thus: her employability). It's a parody, of course: of the way we treat women of a certain age. But unfortunately for the rest of us, we don't get to chug a melted pint of Ben & Jerry's, grow our pubes out, and row off into the sunset. There's no easy way to diffuse gender-based ageism, and what's so damaging about it is just how deeply it's rooted. But the good news is that with age comes confidence: liberation, perhaps, from having to give a shit about what other people think. As for the rest of us—don't forget: we stand on the shoulders of the women who came before us.

The Trap:
"FALLING OFF THE GLASS CLIFF"

Carly Fiorina took over Hewlett-Packard shortly before the tech bubble burst. Anne Mulcahy got a shot at being the first female CEO at Xerox—precisely as the company was being investigated by the SEC. What do these leaders have in common? They are women. Women who were given big responsibilities right as the shit hit the fan. Which meant that when they failed—almost inevitably—the problem was blamed on *them*, not the surrounding circumstances.

It's a psychological phenom known as the "glass cliff," or the idea that women and people of color are more likely to be placed in leadership roles when an organization has a problem, then criticized or ousted (more frequently, and within a shorter time period, than their white male peers) when they fail to fix that problem. The studies of the glass cliff look only at executive women, but it's possible to see how this trap could apply to more junior staffers as well. The sales guys couldn't figure out the lunch order, and now everyone's starving and cranky? Have a woman fix it! Is the marketing report a mess? Bring in a woman! Not only can a woman signal a shift in direction for a troubled task, but we ladies are *really* good at cleaning up other people's messes (amiright?). And when we don't ace the assignment—well, duh—blame the problem on *us*, not the troubling context.

THE HACK

🤜 Bring a Parachute

Be the driver of this bus, not the person under it. Take responsibility for errors that happen under your watch—but *do not* take responsibility for those that don't. Research shows that women are more likely to take the fall anyway; we are judged more harshly than our male counterparts when things go wrong; we're considered "good" at taking the blame because we're female. Do not give in. Negotiate clear metrics ahead of any job or assignment so that you know *exactly* what you're expected to accomplish. Keep detailed evidence—notes, stats, emails—that can be used to tell the *real* story of just what happened, and keep in mind: some of that evidence may need to *pre*date you (call it the Chris Christie approach: "You shoulda seen the place *when I got here*"). The more objective, quantifiable data you collect, the more you can create an airtight self-defense in the event of "failure." And if failure does happen, focus on solutions: "Yeah, this thing happened, this is why, and here's how we're fixing it."

BIG GIRLS DON'T CRY?

Clearly that song was written by a man.

"New rules. You CAN cry at work—in fact, you must cry at work. In fact . . . do me a favor and think of it as 'bring your tears to work day.' Hell, while you're at it, '#bringyourpussytoworkday,' every day. You're gonna need it."

— Jill Soloway, creator of *Transparent*

Here are a few places I have recently cried:

- In bed. You know that one.

- In the bathroom of my coworking office, crouched on the floor.

- In a payphone stall that reeked of pee.

- In front of the mirror trying to put on makeup, but crying every time the mascara wand hit my eye, resulting in smeared black streaks that looked sort of dark and sexy.

- While watching a YouTube clip I later realized was *branded content* for Microsoft. Now I'm more depressed.

- On every form of public transportation: planes, cars, trains, subways, the bus, taxi. Also walking and biking.

- Outside my therapist's office, which is next door to an STD clinic, which always felt like a very public statement.

- In the shower, sitting down, wondering if I was going to get some kind of terrible vaginal infection from touching the porcelain.

Naturally, because I am apparently not only a frequent crier (I had a bad breakup, K?) but also a professional journalist, I started noticing and keeping notes on everything I could find out about crying. Where people cried publicly. Whether people stared at them when they did. Where it was socially acceptable to cry. The history of crying (did you know humans are one of the only species to cry emotional tears?). And, of course, the endless debate over whether or not it's appropriate for women to do it at work.

There's a whole lot of "advice" out there on the topic: most of it speculative, little of it backed up by data, most of it telling you to avoid the tears if you don't want to come off like a total sap. "If anything, when you cry, you give away power," said the TV host Mika Brzezinski, recalling to the *Huffington Post* back in 2014 how she cried when she got fired from CBS. Or as Frances Hesselbein, former CEO of the Girl Scouts, put it: "Tears belong within the family."

But do they?

There's a bit of ancient history of it being socially acceptable for *men* to cry: religious tears, heroic tears, tears of patriotic fervor (members of the British Parliament were said to cry so hard they could barely speak). Yet it's *women's* tears that are viewed as problematic: manipulative (as the Latin writer Pubilius Syrus observed: "Women have learned to shed tears in order that they might lie the better"); as a tool in a woman's arsenal of feminine wiles ("A woman wears her tears like jewelry," an ancient proverb proclaimed); or as a sign that we can't handle the pressures of power.

These days, we still can't win. Cry too much and you're too emotional, soft, your intellect and business acumen clouded by emotion. But if something sad happens and you *don't* cry . . . yikes. Stone cold bitch. If you can fall somewhere in between . . . well, Hillary Clinton accomplished that . . . *once*. When she teared up in New Hampshire in 2008, after being asked how she was holding up, she won the state. More than one pundit attributed the win to her "uncharacteristic" display of emotion.

But it's safe to say that was a fluke. That somehow, by accident, Hillary hit the near-impossible bull's-eye of what falls within the boundaries of "socially acceptable" female crying (which has actually been studied). Among the characteristics: She was crying but not sobbing; shedding a tear, but no more than a tear or two. She was *technically* at work—she is a politician, after all—but her emotion was not *about* work as much as it was about something *personal*. It was also over quickly; she wasn't doing it in a meeting or a performance review (phew!); and she hadn't been set off by immediate work pressure (or a disagreement with a colleague).

Those things may be, ahem, a bit hard to accomplish if you're in the moment, which is why there's plenty of advice on how to allegedly *stop* yourself from crying: jutting out your jaw, chewing gum, drinking water, pinching yourself (really?), or even doing push-ups. Ok, but *actually* what that means is that we end up running to the bathroom or crouching in a stairwell. Putting on sunglasses or pretending we were in the rain. Blaming our allergies. Or we simply run outside and do what my friend Alfia calls "blinking one out"—real quick-like—before walking back in and pretending like nothing happened.

Or . . . here's a wild idea: we could just fucking *cry*.

We could cry, because sometimes it happens, because everyone can get over it, because we're grown-ass professional women who have good work to stand on, and because the other women in our office have most definitely hid in the bathroom crying too.*

We could cry because crying is *good* for you: it lowers cholesterol and helps high blood pressure, boosting your immune system *and* your mood. We could cry because, while the frequency with which we cry may be culturally ingrained—when boys and girls are young, they cry equally, which may lead us to believe that it's only *after* boys learn they aren't *supposed* to cry that they do it less—it doesn't really matter, we still do it more. (According to William Frey, tear researcher—yes, that's a thing!—women cry four times as often as men, an average of five times per month. They also cry for longer lengths of time.)

We could cry because—guess what—our fucking *tear ducts* are anatomically shallower, leading to spillover, which makes our crying more *visible* (and, one might assume, a hell of a lot harder to suppress).

Or we could cry because crying is sometimes our way of expressing frustration, and because work can be frustrating, and because when *men* get frustrated at work they get *angry*—and nobody writes articles about *that*.

So, yes cry I tell you. Cry publicly! Here are a few favorite spots to do it.

---

* TV pilot idea, from my friend Hillary Buckholtz: Talk show, Oprah style, held in the bathroom stalls of corporate offices. No booking producer required—just walk in at any moment and find a woman weeping on a toilet seat (the handicap stall, usually). Hillary is available for hire.

An FFC Analysis:
BEST SPOTS TO CRY PUBLICLY

PARADES

LGBT Pride Parade. Thanksgiving Day Parade. Fourth of July. Puerto Rican Day Parade. "Name it and I'm on the sidelines, wearing sunglasses and inconspicuously wiping tears from my face," says Sarah Jayne, a start-up founder. If you happen to pass one on your way to work, embrace the moment.

PUBLIC TRANSPORTATION

"Airplanes seem especially romantic, but trains can be great too, " one friend tells me. "I ended a six-year relationship and then jumped on a New Jersey Transit train and sobbed so hard I couldn't breathe. Nobody even seemed to notice!"

THE GYM

Tears at the gym are flowing freely these days, complete with choreographed crescendos to go along with your watercycle. "I've had classes where people are literally on all fours sobbing," Taryn Toomey, a fashion exec turned fitness instructor, recently told me. "It's happening everywhere." So hop on a treadmill or head to your closest SoulCycle and sob your heart out.

IN YOGA (OR, BETTER: HOT YOGA)

"Deep hip openers are meant to stir our emotions, as yogis believe that our collected emotional baggage lives in our hips," says yoga instructor Kristin Esposito. And if it's hot yoga? Even better. You're basically sweating out of your eyes already.

PUBLIC MONUMENTS

A great place to pretend you're simply overcome by patriotic fervor, if you happen to have one within walking distance of your desk.*

YOUR CAR

"I am quite envious of people who live in a driving city like Los Angeles where they can enjoy the 'cruising down the 405 highway' kind of cry we all dream about," says Kerry O'Brien, the curator of the *NYC Crying Guide,* a blog that is pretty much what it sounds like—a guide to places to cry in New York City. (If you don't know it already, check it out: cryingnewyork.tumblr.com.)

IN THE SHOWER

Perhaps the most romantic of cry locations, and though it won't help you if you feel a cry coming on in public, it does afford a certain emo vibe. The goal: be the album cover for your own misery.

* Though be warned: you'll likely be crying at the feet of a man. In 2011, of the 5,193 public outdoor sculptures in the United States, only 394, or fewer than 8 percent, were women.

Part Four

GET YOUR SPEAK ON

Ov: The ClusterFuck of SPEAKING WHILE FEMALE

Bill Hoogterp has a drinking game he wants me to try. He says to pick my favorite soda, pour it into a glass halfway, then fill the other half with water. "Taste it," he says, on a break from a speech-coaching workshop he's hosting in New York. I do. It's gross, like a soda that's been sitting overnight with ice.

Watered-down Pepsi is what we sound like, Bill explains, when we pepper our sentences with weak language like "like" and "um." It dilutes what we're saying. So for the next fifteen minutes, every time I use weak language—"like," "ya know," "whatever," "so," "totally," "just," "I mean" (in other words, *my entire vocabulary*)—I must drink. "I'm not sure I like this—" I begin. *Drink!* (The filler phrase: "I'm not sure.") "Wait, but what constitutes filler—" *Drink!* (The filler word in this case: "wait.") "Ah, man, this is like . . ." I stop myself before I have to drink again.

Bill tells me that the most powerful thing a person can do to improve the way they communicate is to eliminate watery language. "It would also make our meetings half as long," he adds.

Bill is the founder of an organization called Own the Room, which has coached the likes of Molly Ringwald (actress), Mellody Hobson (chair of the board at Dreamworks), and Sheryl Sandberg (author of

Lean In) in the art of public speaking (along with the body language to do it well). Since founding the organization with his wife, a former engineer, he's traveled around the globe conducting workshops for women and men at hundreds of international companies. He didn't start out his career in public speaking, but rather as an activist—until he realized how much more effective he could be if he learned how better to project his voice (and message).

" SORRY TO INTERRUPT, & THIS IS
PROBABLY DUMB, BUT, LIKE I'M
PRETTY SURE THAT WELL-BEHAVED
WOMEN SELDOM MAKE HISTORY."

— the historian LAUREL THATCHER ULRICH,
reimagined as a millennial office worker

I ask Bill to assess my speaking style on the spot, and he directs me to describe what I do for a living into his iPhone. He observes closely, and then we watch the video together. "Do you want the honest version or the brutally honest version?" he asks me. I tell him to be brutal. "You have really good micropauses." (I am flattered, though I have no idea what a micropause is.) "You use almost none of your volume range, but your speed range is good. You don't use upspeak. But you don't have authoritative speak, either."

He pauses. "Do you want to know what your problem is?" he asks.

"Uh, *yes*," I tell him, employing yet another filler word.

"Your problem is you're driving a Ferrari with the handbrake on. You're capable of more power than you realize."

If the goal is succinctness, then Bill is right: I probably *could* convey more power if I cut the filler. And yet, I sort of *like* the way I talk. Should I have to change it, simply because it doesn't fit with what's been deemed, somewhat arbitrarily, the workplace standard?

At a time when dissecting the way women speak has seemingly become a favorite pastime—our pitch, our sorrys, even our punctuation—Bill is part of a growing field of coaches and consultants who teach people how to deliver a message effectively: to open their throats, to create more oral resonance, to cut filler words, to use space and body language to convey authority and add gravitas.

When it comes to women and speech, though, there's an important caveat—that what's been deemed the *ideal* doesn't necessarily match the way women actually, well, *talk*. And so we are told that we sound unconfident when we raise our pitch. That we should remove our "likes" and "justs" (and there are apps to help us do it), de-fry our chords, and that we should practice, and learn to find our "best speaking voices."

But what if we've already found them?

Linguists will tell you clearly: male and female speech patterns have always differed. Women tend to have more versatile intonation patterns; they place more emphasis on certain words; they speak about more personal topics. And while the masculine style of communication at work is to give orders—as in, "Here's what we need to do" or "We have to do better"—the feminine style is to persuade. "I have an idea that I want you to consider." Or she may phrase her idea as a question: "What do you think of this approach?"

It has long been a truism that women lead *popular* linguistic trends: creating new words, playing around with sounds, creating verbal shortcuts that catch on in the vernacular (pretty sure it wasn't a man who first LOLed). Yet it is the masculine style of speech—succinct, straightforward, confident—that is associated with *workplace* leadership and power. Which means that when it comes to work, women are often left to adapt their language to speak more like *men:* female speech is perceived as insecure, less competent, and sometimes even less trustworthy. No wonder Margaret Thatcher hired a vocal coach to help her sound less "shrill."

But wait, there's more. Yes, women can adapt, but they mustn't adapt *too* much—lest they sound masculine. In her book, *Talking from 9 to 5,* linguist Deborah Tannen describes a woman who received negative feedback when she tried to talk like her male peers—but was able to remedy the situation by adding words like "sorry" back into her speech. As Tannen noted later: How could anybody possibly *not* lack confidence if she's constantly being told she's doing everything wrong?

And so here we go again . . . that persistent double standard, that *damned if you do, damned if you don't,* speaking softly when they're trying to talk loudly, trying to cut the sorrys while still sounding modest, avoiding "I feel like" but still speaking in a nurturing tone. Easy, right?!

At the end of the day, there is no right way to talk—especially if you want to sound like, yourself. But there are some common tripwires you may want to approach with caution.

Verbal Tripwire:
THE OVER-APOLOGIZER

A brief list of the most idiotic apologies I've recently issued:

- A "sorry, it was a latte" to the barista at my local coffee shop, who *always* gets my order wrong, whom I *always* tip, and whom I had to correct when—once again—he gave me the wrong drink.

- An "Oh my gosh, I'm so sorry!" to the guy who bumped into me walking down the street, causing me to spill said coffee.

- An "I'm so sorry for all the back and forth" to the sort-of-colleague I was meeting after picking up my coffee, for having to reschedule once—which I was actually not remotely sorry for at all.

"I realized my 'sorry' habit was bad when I heard myself apologizing to my boyfriend for a burned dinner that *he* cooked," my friend Cristen Conger, the host of a podcast called *Stuff Mom Never Told You,* mused recently. I was working on a column about women and apologies and had asked her if she ever overindulged. I forwarded her response to another friend. "What's up with ladies and 'I'm sorry'?" I wrote.

"Sorry I didn't reply sooner," she replied, forty-five minutes later.

Once upon a time, the word "sorry" was reserved for things a person might *actually* be sorry for: spilling wine on the new white silk you'd borrowed without asking; denting your mother's car; screwing something up—like *really* screwing something up—at work. These days it's more like a crutch: a space filler, a hedge, a way to interject, state an opinion, to politely ask without offending, to state an opinion, say "excuse me," or just about anything that involves speaking up or stating an opinion at all.

Can't we even own the apology—or the insult?

There are plenty of times when saying "sorry" actually works. But if your audience is not a prickly individual but a full conference room or a reply-all email list, know this: You may say, "Sorry to interrupt, but I think . . . ," but what you sound like is, "I have zero confidence in my idea—why should you?"

TIMES I APOLOGIZED

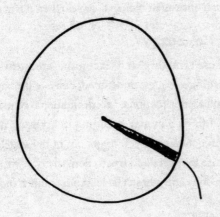

WHEN I'M
ACTUALLY
SORRY

THREAT LEVEL

When You're Actually Sorry

Allow for a moment a refresher on the fundamentals of a well-deployed "sorry." A textbook apology comes when a speaker realizes she has done something harmful or offensive to the addressee and wants to put their relationship back on an even keel. Apology accepted? Great! The relationship can once again flourish, no (further) harm done.

The "Excuse Me" Sorry

In today's off-label use, "I'm sorry" and "excuse me" are attention getters immediately preceding a request or demand; delicate throat clearings to mitigate an unpleasant situation or confrontational request (for instance, "I'm sorry, I think you may be sitting in my seat," meaning a demand: "Yeah, I'm gonna need you to get out of my seat"); and as a euphemistic disguise for anger and frustration, when we expect something to have been done and it hasn't (at least not to our standards).

The Polite Sorry

Yep, sometimes "I'm sorry" is simply a "linguistic tip of the hat," as Tannen calls it, one of many social niceties that help conversation flow. When you want someone to clarify what she said: "I'm sorry, I'm not sure what you mean." When you are interrupting others to ask a question: "Oh I'm sorry, I'm looking for so-and-so, have you seen him?" British natives—men as well as women—use "sorry" in this way all the time, Tannen notes, yet no one thinks it reveals insecurity or dooms them to a bleak future.

Verbal Tripwire:
UPSPEAK?

"I first noticed the trend among my very smart undergraduate female students," Thomas Linneman, a sociology professor at the College of William and Mary, was recently quoted saying. "They'd get up in front of the class and say, 'These are my results? Here's what I found?' It was out of control."

It's called upspeak, and when it doesn't involve turning a statement into a question ("Yes, I'm sure?"), it involves adding a question to the end of a statement ("You know what I mean?" "Does that make sense?"). Both women and men do it (George W. Bush was known for it), but women do it more often than men; white women do it the most; and in one study, of *Jeopardy* contestants, researchers found that the more successful a female contestant became, the more she did it, while the opposite was true for men.

"They misunderestimated me?"

GEORGE W. BUSH

THREAT LEVEL

To Stop a Manterrupter

There's at least one bit of research that finds some may use uptalk as a defense mechanism to prevent others from cutting you off. (Remember, women are twice as likely to be interrupted.) Turns out that questioning tone in your voice might actually be good for something: it indicates you're not yet finished.

To Check In

As if to say, "Are you still with me? Are you paying attention here?"

To Elicit Affirmation

Affirmation is nice, and sometimes a questioning tone will elicit words of encouragement: "Totally!" "Yes, I agree." But if your intent is to actually impress your listener, it seems ma-a-a-aybe a teensy bit unwise to present your statement in a way where you possibly sorta undermine yourself . . . ahem. You know what I mean?

To Convey Confidence

In *Talking from 9 to 5,* Deborah Tannen describes a male CEO who explains that he often has to make decisions "in five minutes" about projects on which his staff may have worked five months. He uses this rule: if the person making the proposal seems confident, he approves it. Ending your statements in a question or, for that matter, beginning them with an apology? The opposite of confident.

Verbal Tripwire:
HEDGING

HEDGE WORDS (Don't be a hog!)

QUALIFIERS	FILLERS	TAGS	WARM-UP WORDS
- I'm not sure if this is right, but ...	- um - like - Kind of - Apparently	- Does that make sense?	- Just - Actually

They're called "hedges," and they come in many forms. There's the trembling qualifier ("I'm not sure if this is right, but . . ."), serving to counteract the fear that a statement might actually be wrong. There are filler words like "kind of," "sort of," "apparently," "supposedly," and so on, adverbs with just the tiniest hint of an opinion. There are the attempts at confirmation called "tags" ("Does that make sense?"), as well as sneaky disagreements ("*Actually,* that's not right") and warm-up words like "just" ("I just wanted to check in . . .").

Think of these words as a kind of performative maybes, with seven A's and three E's (maaaaaaaybeee). They are permission words: used to lessen the impact of an utterance or qualify a statement to make you sound equivocal. While kin to "sorry," this category is different—in that it's not a direct apology so much as apologetic air-stirring, a shy knock on a door, or as former Google exec Ellen Petry Leanse described it, a way to "put the conversation partner into the 'parent' position, granting them more authority and control."

She is right: technically our statements *would* sound more assertive if we removed both the "but" and the qualifier preceding it. BUT! Perhaps this is the very reason *why* we use qualifiers to begin with: to sound less assertive, softer, less pushy, less demanding. To create the effect of a thought we both, speaker and listener, have arrived at together.

THREAT LEVEL

For Emphasis

"That meeting was *just* terrible." "That meal was *just* wonderful." Those "justs" aren't uncertain, they're emphatic.

To Make a Request

"What if we *maybe* stop by for a minute?" "Could I *possibly* ask you a couple of questions?"

To Buy Time

A well-deployed "um" or "you know" can give you a moment for your brain to collect your thoughts—another version of the time-tested "That's a good question, *Bob*," which manages to somehow balance condescension and compliment in one.

The Confident Swagger Hedge

Used in office scenarios to actually *make up for the fact* that you don't have an answer, while still managing to give an opinion. "Well, I don't know who *has the time* to know everything about [insert topic at hand]—but it's my feeling that we should [insert opinion anyway]." If you can employ it, use it. Men do it all the time.

The Aggressive "Actually"

It's the "talk to the hand" of the adverb world, as the journalist Jen Doll put it: a sneaky word, used to say "you're right, I'm right" but without *actually* owning the correction. Consider: "Hi, Jennifer." *"Actually,* it's Jessica." Or "The team is all here." "Actually, we're waiting for Ashley." "Actually" can lessen the blow, but it can also be used to deliver a powerful bomb. "The numbers are down sixteen percent." "No, ACTUALLY, they're up by five." Just don't let it sound like you're surprised by your own conviction.

Verbal Tripwire:
HOUSTON, I *FEEL* LIKE WE HAVE A PROBLEM

There was a time when "I feel" might have indicated that you actually, you know, *felt* something—like sick, excited, or guilty. But these days feelings seem to have become a touchy-feely, less direct way of stating an opinion—"I feel like we should consider trying X," or simply another way of saying "I think" or "I believe."

"I feel like" started catching on in the 1970s (an era of all *sorts* of feelings) but really gained traction in the early 2000s—like most things linguistic, among young women. It made sense: many of these speech patterns go back to our very adolescence, when girls make friends based on *sharing* (secrets, stories, *feelings*), while boys tend to play in groups, shouting commands. (No feels there.) As we grow up, though, we seem to continue to engage in these playground speech patterns—and for women, we strangely do it *more* when there are men around, peppering our language with oh-so-many feels.

There are cases when expressing these feelings can be useful: there is less risk in saying "I feel like" than there is in saying "I know" or "I believe" (and in some cases we can use that nuance to our advantage). But how much of "I feel" has to do with the expectation that women must play the nurturing, *feeling* role and cannot simply be direct? We're talking about business here—not a couple's therapy sesh. "At work, it's wimpy, weak and wishy-washy," writes Phyllis Mindell, a professor at Georgetown, in *How to Say It for Women*. "Describing events or issues in terms of 'feelings' substitutes 'psychobabble' for clear thought."

THREAT LEVEL

To Be Polite

Sure, instead of saying "I feel like you're not understanding" you could say "You're *not* understanding"—but "I feel like" softens the blow.

To Resolve Conflict

If you make it about your *feelings,* it's less likely to feel like an attack. Consider: "I feel frustrated with your progress" or "I'm disappointed in your performance." It's true that women suffer if they're perceived as *too* emotional at work. But there is also research to prove that expressing "muted" emotions at work, such as "I feel," can be an incredibly effective way to communicate. It's when these feels cross the threshold into "deviant"—crying, yelling, clearly angry—that women are penalized.

Public Speeches

All those feels are taking away from the time you have *to actually make your point.*

Verbal Tripwire:
LIKE, EEOW. MOI. GAWWWWWD.

"You sound like a Valley girl," the man on the phone told me. "How old are you—thirteen?"

I wasn't thirteen but twenty-four. And I wasn't from the Valley, but calling from the New York office of an investigative journalist I worked for. The man on the other end was a high-level city official (also a dick, apparently) and I was mortified. From that moment forward, I became self-conscious about my voice.

Valley girl speak, as the *like, totally, for real, seriously, omg*-laced speech is known, has ostensibly been around since the 1970s—observed as a kind of dialect adopted by young white women from the San Fernando Valley (outside Los Angeles). But it wasn't until the 1980s that the concept grew to a full-fledged cultural phenom, parroted in a Frank Zappa song featuring the Valley-talking voice of his young daughter.

"Like, oh my God."

"Like totally."

"I like love going into like clothing stores and stuff."

In the 1990s, Valley girl speak—and the fashion and attitude that went along with it—was parodied in the *way existential* feminist masterpiece *Clueless,* a reimagined portrayal of Jane Austen's *Emma.* In *Clueless,* the Valley-talking Cher (Alicia Silverstone) and her best friend Dionne (Stacey Dash) navigate high school and everything it entails: social status, friendships, sex.

These days, Valleyspeak isn't limited to women of the Valley (or women at all: at least one researcher has found that *men* use "like" more than women), yet the image of a schoolgirl-skirt-clad Cher, tossing "As ifs!" to any guy who crossed her path, remains. Along with it the stereotype: dumb, immature, mall shopping, shallow.

THREAT LEVEL

We're, Like, Evolved, OK?

That's the argument of the linguist Robin Lakoff, who advises that much of the same Valleyspeak we see criticized is actually a sign of an evolved way of communicating that sends signals to a listener. Elements of this speech can engage, they can make people feel included, they can even build trust. "They create cohesion and coherence," Lakoff has said. "This is the major job of an articulate social species. If women use these forms more, it is because we are better at being human." Boo-yah.

"Like" in Place of "Said"

Know the difference: "like" as a *filler* ("I'm, like, totally starved") and "like" in place of "said" or "for example" ("And then he was like, 'We'd be happy to give you that raise'" or "Let's find a way to solve this problem, like taking the client to lunch").

First Impressions

What we know for sure about Valleyspeak is that your parents, or your nonmillennial colleagues, probably don't get it. (But let's not forget: they had their own groovy speech patterns.) Like it or not, people make judgments based on superficial things—such as the *way* you talk instead of what you're saying. So until you've had the chance to show that you *do* know what you're talking about, proceed with caution.

Verbal Tripwire:
TALKING LIKE A SEXY BAAABBBYY

Kim Kardashian has made a fortune off of it, but most of us won't. She's the woman who ends her calls with "Thank yewwwwwwww"; who pads her authority with a creaky tone. That precise tone is called "vocal fry"—the low-octave rasp or fry-like sizzle achieved by vocal folds rubbing together all weird, and it is done by both women and men. And sure, that soft pitch may sound kinda sexy, it can be useful for emphasis, and it's kinda fun to do, but leadership—for better or worse—is associated with more resonant, authoritative, and unfried tones.

> **vo-cal fry / n.**
> An awesome name for a feminist band, but more commonly used to describe a style of speech that involves elongating vowels, i.e., hiiiiiiiiii or thank youuuuuuu. Also known as "creaky voice."

The media has been churning out trend pieces on vocal fry—or "creaky voice," as it's also known—since at least 2011, when young women (allegedly) began adopting it to emulate the Kardashians of the world and were being dinged for it at work (deemed less competent, less educated, less trustworthy, less attractive, and less hirable, at least according to one hotly debated study). In reality, vocal fry dates back to at least 1964, when it was used by British men to—get this—convey their *superior* social standing. It gained popularity in the United States around 2003, first observed among female speakers of a Chicano dialect in California.

In its more current iteration, though, there is one glaring problem: while both women and men do it, it is only women who seem to suffer for it. Part of that may have a scientific explanation—fry is associated with a sudden decrease in sound, says the NYU linguist Lisa Davidson. Because men's voices are generally lower in pitch, that shift may be less noticeable. Of course, fry is *also* considered by many linguists to be an attempted *antidote* to upspeak (that tendency to end your statements in a question, with a high-pitched rise). So in effect, we're combating the inflection by trying to deepen our voices, but then arriving at a vocal fry register. Can't win, right?

THREAT LEVEL

Anybody Under 40

Really. Amid all the hoopla over vocal fry, a Stanford linguist decided to poll her students on whether they, like her, found the sound of it grating. They didn't. She duplicated that premise in a larger study of five hundred adults—and determined that it was only *those over forty* who were bugged by vocal fry. In which case: curb the fry or don't, but soon enough, fry may be the vocal norm.

In Meetings, Interviews

A 2014 study staged mock job interviews in which the researchers recorded seven men and seven women saying "Thank you for considering me for this opportunity" in both their normal voice and in vocal fry—then asked study participants to rate them. The sample size was tiny, but what they found was that compared to a fry-free speaking voice, frying female voices connoted a speaker who was dumber, less skilled, and less attractive to the listener—and it was women, not men, who were the most critical.

Saying Effffff Off

In the incredibly satisfying but dangerous category: telling people to *get the eff over it* and going about your day talking however you damn well please.

Verbal Tripwire:
THE OFFICE XO-ER

It was a friendly call to get to know each other, the kind any two thirty-something professionals might have. A colleague had put my friend Amanda in touch with a producer in LA. They chatted about their respective creative projects, and how they might collaborate down the line. They said they'd follow up.

Amanda woke up the next morning to a message from the woman. "Absolutely LOVED talking," she had written, followed by XOXO.

That was nice, Amanda thought. She figured she'd reply later. But before she had the chance, there was another follow-up. "XO," the subject line read. She clicked. There was just one line:

XOXOXOXOXOXOXOXOXO

Amanda was mystified. "I'd never seen so many hugs or kisses in any kind of correspondence, even from my parents or boyfriends," she said. "In which case: Was this person actually in love with me? And if I didn't respond with equal love, was it going to hurt her feelings?"

I called up a linguist to ask about the origins of "XO"—which apparently dates back to at least 1763. Back then though, you used it when you *actually* wanted to send somebody a hug and a kiss. Not simply . . . a person you've spoken with once. And yet, "XO" is employed so routinely today that linguists have studied its use. Guess what they found? Yep, it is largely used by women.

THREAT LEVEL

To Inspire Camaraderie

The "thanks, man" of professional sisterhood.

The Lazy XO

Faster than "I hope you're doing well, it was great talking to you" as a way to sign off an email—but do you mean it?

The Passive-Aggressive XO

"I need this report on my desk and I need it *yesterday*. XOXO"

To Temper a Demand

Think of all those studies concluding that women must be authoritative in the office but also nice. In that context, perhaps XO is a savvy means of navigating a persistent double standard.

Sort-Of-Verbal Tripwire:
EMOJIMANIA

It began about a year ago, with a smiley face here and there, a flexed muscle for encouragement, or hearts when friends would send baby pictures. I particularly enjoyed the "yikes" emoji—that smiling yellow face with the toothy grimace, perfect for "Stuck on the subway!" or "Oy. I just woke up and it's one p.m." It wasn't long before I was replacing words with characters, sending my mother complicated sequences and using a "thumbs-up" to indicate to a friend that I wasn't mad. Then one time I practically burst into tears after spending ten minutes scouring my iPhone for the dancing lady emoji, again and again, as if it had somehow disappeared. I was deep into my search when I got a phone call from a work contact I'd been waiting to speak with. Naturally, I pressed ignore.

The roots of emoticons date back to the 1880s, while the first digitized emoji emerged in 1990s Japan. But in America, the modern explosion has been a distinctly postmillennial trend. And while emoji are by no means *limited* to female usage, like most things linguistic, it's the ladies leading the charge.

THREAT LEVEL

Emojiing Your Boss

If your boss emojis you, don't be afraid to emoji back. This is called "behavioral mimicry," and it can actually build trust.

Emoji as Praise

A 💯 is a great way to say "You aced it!" while the 🔥 is a perfect way to say "That presentation was fire." Also useful for any situation that has a glint of festivity: the dancing lady 💃, which is also, importantly, my mother's favorite emoji.

Rule of Three

Three smiley faces = fun! Four smiley faces = thirsty AF.

Don't Try These at Home

Although you deserve a raise and should absolutely ask for one, the 💰💰 emoji should probably not be used in the process. Similarly, if you happen to be talking shit about your boss—or the Australian foreign minister, describing Vladimir Putin—the red hot devil face 😈 is likely to get you questioned (hopefully not during a Senate committee meeting).

IS THAT DESCRIPTION
▷ SEXIST? ◁

ITS CALLED THE LAW OF REVERSIBILITY
AND IT GOES LIKE THIS

STEP 1: REVERSE THE GENDER OF YOUR SUBJECT

STEP 2: SEE IF IT SOUNDS FUNNY

STEP 3: REPEAT

Don't Be a

DICK-TIONARY
An Almost A–Z Guide

ere are a few words and phrases I wish I could avoid hearing about myself: "Aggressive," for going after a promotion. "Controlling," as said by an ex-boyfriend, when I made household decisions. "Crazy," as I was called by a female editor who didn't like my attitude. "Difficult," when I asked for more money on a magazine assignment. "Bitchy," when I turned down another writer's pitch.

I've been called "emotional" for raising my voice, "hysterical" for getting angry, and a "stalker" for being persistent. I had a (male) colleague who frequently told me "not to worry my pretty little head" and was recently asked by a (female) journalist about my marital status, for an article she was writing about *combating gender bias.*

Most of us don't think much about the subtleties of language. It flows out of our mouths, sometimes we regret it, most of the time we move on. But when it comes to women, words matter more than we might think. Remember in 2008, when a John McCain supporter asked of Hillary Clinton, "How do we beat the bitch?" McCain laughed, quipping awkwardly that it was an "excellent question." But research has shown that even subtly sexist words—not just "bitch," but say, "shrill"—influence voters' likelihood of supporting a candidate, and whether they support female politicians at all.

There once was a guide for this kind of thing, and one I happen to have on my bookshelf, stolen from an old *Newsweek* library where it had been checked out exactly once. It's called *The Handbook of Nonsexist Writing,* by the feminist writers Casey Miller and Kate Swift, and it's full of charming 1980s advice: they traced the evolution of "man," advised on the propriety of "girl" versus "gal," and poked at the question of whether "housewives" should be referred to as "working women" ("What are housewives if not working women?" they asked).

There is no real handbook equivalent today—but there should be. Here's a crib sheet to get you started.

Aggressive

She's called "aggressive," while he's called "assertive"—and yet they exhibit the exact same behaviors.

Ballsy

As in, brave. Why does bravery have to be associated with male anatomy?

Bossy

Which actually means to exhibit boss-like qualities, which you'd think would be a good thing. Except that women are so fearful of being called this word that, according to a Girl Scouts study, young women will actually avoid leadership roles in order to dodge it.

Catfight

Men disagreeing: strong in their convictions, admirable, simply doing business. Women disagreeing: catfight! Hair pulling! Potential for shirts to be torn open! Quick, come watch!

Crazy

A catchall put-down for any woman you don't like/who makes you uncomfortable/who doesn't fit the mold.

Dramatic

Is she *actually* dramatic, or do you perceive her that way because she's female?

Emotional

Or: how women are perceived when they express anger or displeasure at work, while a man who does the same is simply viewed as "passionate."

Feisty

In 1984 Geraldine Ferraro, the first woman on a major party ticket, "was described as 'feisty' and 'pushy but not threatening,' and was asked if she knew how to bake blueberry muffins. When she stood before the Democratic National Convention in San Francisco, anchor Tom Brokaw announced: 'Geraldine Ferraro . . . the first woman to be nominated for vice president . . . size six!'"

Female

When Shonda Rhimes was sent a draft of a press release for an event she was set to headline—calling her "the most powerful black female showrunner in Hollywood"—she crossed out "female" and "black" and sent it back. When we can remove qualifiers from these superlative phrases—because nobody would ever call somebody the "most powerful *white male showrunner*"—then our work here will be done.

Girls

Great for talking about your girl gang. But if you are in a professional setting, and you're speaking about a woman, and you're not referencing the HBO series, please *try* to call us women.

"Having It All"

Can Wendy Davis have it all? Can Carly Fiorina? What about Shonda Rhimes? And while we're at it, how do these women *do* it all? Tina Fey has declared this "the rudest question you can ask a woman," and its answer is simple: we're doing it the same way a dude would, except that he doesn't have to answer questions.

He

Do you use "he" when really you mean "person"? Alternatives include "they," "she or he," and "one."

Icy

An appropriate way to describe a brisk winter day, not the personality of a woman.

Kiddo

A word that you should never call a woman in a professional environment no matter how cute and youthful she is.

Ladylike

Or its younger sister: Girly. What makes somebody ladylike, anyway? If these terms don't tell us something about a subject beyond the fact that she is *female*, it's safe to assume they are sexist filler.

Man
In the sense of chair*man,* spokes*man,* fire*man* when really this person could be male or female..

Mistress
She's a mistress, and he's . . . what, a player who had an affair?

Mrs.
"Mr." doesn't communicate whether or not a man is "taken," so how 'bout we try "Ms." (or even "Mx.")

Nag
A word reserved for a woman who asks twice.

Nice
It's nice that you think she's nice. But what about an adjective with more *there* there? "The problem with nice," says Robin Lakoff, "is that women have to be it . . . or else."

Perky
"You're not perky enough for me," the writer Gay Talese once told a female teaching assistant, after she declined to make him tea. Tea request aside, serious question: Have you ever met a man who was expected to be perky?

Pretty
And other physical descriptions you should avoid using when actually trying to describe a woman's qualifications. By which I mean cleavage, cankles, haircuts, pantsuits, whether she is blond, blue-eyed, or petite—all irrelevant to a woman's abilities.

Psycho
See CRAZY.

Questions
We're talking here about mindboggling idiotic inquiries you'd never put to a man. Such as: Will spaceflight affect your reproductive organs? What do you wear to the gym? Will hormones affect your ability to do the job?

Sassy
Or, she who dares to express an opinion.

Seminal
Because works of great importance must come from a man's crotch. (No, really, the linguistic origin of this word is *semen*.)

Shrill
A word that—along with sisters "shrieking" and "screeching"—is used twice as often to refer to women than men. It is true that women naturally have higher-pitched voices than men.

Slut
She's a slut, he's a stud. Double-standard alert!

Testy
I've never heard a man called testy, have you?

Uppity
A word applied to women, and often black women, who speak their minds.

Vagina

All hail the vagina!! A great word—except when it's sister P-word is used to refer to somebody who's "weak." If there is one thing that is the opposite of weak, it is the vagina. You try pushing a baby out of one.

Work-Life Balance

Or a nonsense term based on some sort of archaic idea about what it means to compartmentalize your life into work and home. In short: impossible.

Yappy

To talk at length in an annoying way. The stereotype: that it's women who are doing most of the yapping. The truth: when women and men are together, it's men who do most of the talking. Put that in your pipe and smoke it.

Part Five

F YOU, PAY ME

A Negotiation CHEAT SHEET

(Tear It Out and Stuff It in Your Bra)

I automatically feel dirty asking for money."

They were the words of a female writer, seated in a Manhattan living room, explaining to a group of female friends that she was trying to muster the courage to ask an editor for a contract.

"I want to be paid for my writing, but I find myself thinking, 'I'm just a lousy writer,'" she said. "When it comes to money, I feel I'm worthless." The woman speaking could have been a younger version of myself—and yet the conversation wasn't happening among my Fight Club, but a consciousness-raising group from 1970, recorded in the *New York Times*. Ah, how little has changed.

 I first negotiated a salary after finding out what a male friend doing a similar job was making—and that it was thousands (tens of thousands, actually) more than what I made. I didn't get slipped an anonymous note telling me I made less (what happened to Lily Ledbetter, the Goodyear employee for whom the Fair Pay Act is named). It was really more benign. I just asked him one day when we were talking about our jobs, and he told me. When he realized how much less I was making, he encouraged me to ask for more.

Still, I'd never asked for a raise before, and the idea was daunting. Negotiation is not a skill we are taught in school. So I started making lists, documenting every accomplishment I could think of. I asked editors who liked my work to vouch for me. I edited and re-edited my list. Then I forced myself to email my boss, asking him for a meeting to discuss "my future." For the next six hours, I checked my email obsessively while convincing myself that I shouldn't have done it. *What if he said no? What if he thought I was presumptuous? What if he just never responded?*

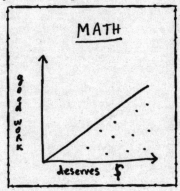

There's no easy way around it: negotiating sucks. It's difficult, anxiety-inducing, awkward, risky—no matter your gender. Some people are good at it, a few freaks may even enjoy it, but most people I know would rather do almost *anything* else (and in fact we often do avoid it, at great cost).

But negotiating *as a woman* is a whole other story. We may be comfortable talking about our bathroom habits and orgasms, but when it comes to money, we suddenly clam up. That, and we face an absurd maze of challenges—with even the best advice at times requiring us to *conform* to gender stereotypes (you know, like . . . smile!).

I got my raise that first time I asked, but negotiating has never gotten any easier. I just *don't like doing it*. But I've done enough research at this point to know that I have to—and that there are some simple tactics every woman can stockpile (including knowing that women are better at negotiating when we're told it's OK to do so—so here I am, telling you it's OK!).

Don't take my negotiation advice because I'm a good negotiator. Take it because I'm a shitty one—which means I've parsed the literature, obsessively, to learn how to get better.

STOP MAKING EXCUSES

Oh yeah, I know this game. Excuses like:

- I'm leaving anyway.

- It's not the right time.

- I'm not sure what I want.

- I'm bad at negotiating.

- The company's not doing so well.

- That person hates me.

- I don't want to get rejected.

- I didn't do a good enough job.

If you do *not* see your excuse of choice listed here, that's OK. Whatever the excuse, ask yourself: If I do this—despite all of the very convincing reasons I am telling myself I shouldn't—what is the absolute worst thing that can happen? I'm going to answer this question for you: it's that your boss says no. And what are you going to *do* if your boss says no? I'll give you three options: You can say you're disappointed, ask what you can do to improve, and make a plan to check in again in six months. You can do that *and* start looking for a new job. Or you can quit. Whatever you choose, none of these options is the end of the world. Now stop making excuses.

WHAT YOU'RE UP AGAINST

The Wage Gap Is Real

In America today, full-time working women make seventy-nine cents to the male dollar on average. When broken down by race, African-American women make sixty-four cents and Hispanics make fifty-four. There are lots of arguments about this number—primarily, that it doesn't account for job choice, or women taking time off to care for children. Both of these things are true. But you know what? Even when you *do* account for job choice, and compare *childless* women and men who have graduated from the *same* colleges, and control for things like GPA, hours worked, and taking time off, this gap persists: in their first year out of college, women will earn just 93 percent of what their male peers do.

THE WAGE GAP IN AMERICA

WHITE MAN $1   WHITE WOMAN 78 cents   BLACK WOMAN 64 cents   HISPANIC WOMAN 54 cents

Women Don't Ask

Yup: humans of the female persuasion are a quarter as likely as men to negotiate a salary, and they ask for less money when they do, despite research showing that employees who negotiate are promoted seventeen months sooner than those who don't. Not asking doesn't just contribute to the wage gap. You could argue that it contributes to the bias that prevents women from asking in the first place.

Women Who Ask are "Pushy"

Women who negotiate are more likely to be viewed as pushy—and, in some cases, less likely to get the job.

Beware the Bluffer

Women are more often lied to during negotiations than men—by both women and men. As in: "We just don't have the budget right now" or "Now is not a good time," when it's really as good a time as any. It's interesting to note that while both men and women lie frequently, research has found (more generally) that women are likely to lie to spare feelings, while men lie to save money, win an argument, or get something they want—all things that come into play in a negotiation. Try to be sharp eared in your conversations—what rings false? Be prepared to (respectfully) challenge responses that sound fishy.

LAY THE GROUNDWORK

Keep a List

A negotiation is the one time you can actually hand over a piece of paper (or follow up with an email later) with everything you've accomplished. Consider including the following:

- Ways you've contributed to your company's profit or image
- Specific examples of *how* you contributed
- Data that *prove* that contribution—be it a sales report or an email from a boss or customer telling you that you did a great job, or something else

Get Colleagues on Your Side

Reach out to all the people who have a stake in your negotiation. Will they be willing to advocate on your behalf after you've made your ask? Will they give you a positive review if your boss asks them? These people may not play an active role, but think of them as your backup if a negotiation gets tense.

Know the Going Rate

You may not feel comfortable asking a colleague what they make (and it may go against your company policy to do so). But find out some basics about the going rate so you don't throw out something that's absurd (when in doubt try Glassdoor, PayScale, or Salary.com). Research from Linda Babcock and Hannah Riley Bowles, professors at Carnegie Mellon and Harvard, respectively, has found that women are more successful in negotiations when there's less ambiguity about the appropriate standards—so any frame of reference, industry wide or within your own company, can help you make your case.

Plan When You Want to Ask

You can't just hit up your boss for a raise whenever you feel like it, so choose your timing wisely. Don't negotiate when you're feeling resentful or angry about a situation at work. Likewise, take a moment to think about your manager's ideal frame of mind (no cornering her in the ladies' room). The best time, naturally, is right after you've done something awesome. It's even better if that awesome thing happens to correspond with your annual review (or a similar check-in). If it doesn't, do you have a review time scheduled already? Could this wait until then? Consider your options.

Know What You're Asking For

Be sure that you have a concrete "ask"—a dollar amount, an exact title, a benefit—in the back of your mind before you go in. You may not need to use this number, but what we're trying to avoid here is you shrugging your shoulders when you're asked what you want. Don't give up your power because you don't know what you're asking for. Your employer will happily make the decision for you.

SET UP THE MEETING

Do not bust in on your boss mid-bologna sandwich and begin freneti-cally making your case. Approach the person with whom you want to have the conversation and set up a time *in the future* to do it. Women tend to be more nervous than men about the approach, so here are a few things to consider:

- Is it appropriate to reach out over email? Some people find that less nerve-wracking. If so, send a short note asking for a meeting and give a reason for it. You don't have to tell this person you want a raise, but say something like, "I'd like to set up a time to [talk/check in/touch base] about my [progress/review/bonus]."

- Would your boss respond better to an in-person ask? Then figure out a time to walk by their desk.

NEGOTIATION TACTICS FOR EVERYONE

Play the First Card!

Don't be afraid to be the first to disclose a number—and *always* ask for more than you think you'll get. One study found that for every dollar higher a person lays out on the table first translates to about 50 cents more in the final agreement. I like this motto, from ad executive Cindy Gallop: "You should ask for the highest number you can utter without actually bursting out laughing." The goal here is to not leave your employer LOLing too (because you've asked for something so absurd) but starting a negotiation at a higher point will leave you more room to make concessions if you need to.

Negotiate on the Whole, Not the Parts

Keep in mind a negotiation is not always about *just* the money. There're benefits, flexibility, a child-care bonus, vacation, a 401(k), having your employer give you time off to finish a degree, having them *pay* for you to finish your degree. Honestly, you can sometimes make these up. Start big, but have smaller options as well (no, snacks do *not* count as compensation!). Be prepared to present each, and consider ranking them by importance, but keep some in your back pocket should other things fall off the table.

Tailor Your Ask

There's no negotiation advice that's going to work in every scenario with every person, so each step of the way, remember who you're dealing with. When it's time to make your case, do it in a way that takes into account the other person—whether it's the language you use, the way you frame what you've accomplished (according to what you know they value most), or who you need on your side (people they trust) to make it happen.

Anticipate Objections

And be prepared with a response for each. If they say "We've had a tough quarter" or "I'm not sure you're ready for this responsibility" can you make the case otherwise? Even if you're asking for something you know will be difficult, have a smooth answer ready (and check out WTF to Say on pages 209–212 for some responses to specific objections.)

No Bluffing

If you are going in with another job offer: determine *ahead of time* whether or not you're willing to leave if they say no. Don't discount the possibility—if you really don't want to take it—of telling your employer that. ("I have this other offer, I really don't want to take it, so I'm hoping we can reach a place where we're both happy . . .")

Know When to Stop Talking

Put your offer on the table and then shut up. Let them make the next move.

NEGOTIATION TRICKS
FOR WOMEN

Use "We" Not "I"

While women are seen as "pushy" when they negotiate for themselves, it turns out they're successful when they do it on behalf of others—because they don't come off as self-serving. How to accomplish this "on behalf of others" vibe when you're negotiating for yourself? Substitute "we" for "I": "*We* felt really good about *our* accomplishments this year"—followed by how *you* contributed.

Make It About Collaboration

This isn't about a fight for benefits you've been denied; it's about being part of a *team* and working together to come to a mutually beneficial agreement. Remind them: you're on *their side.*

Hedge

Yes, in the same way we are *not* supposed to hedge our language, but research has found that hedging can offset the likability penalty women face when they do negotiate. One script that negotiation expert Hannah Riley Bowles suggests: "I don't know how typical it is for people at my level to negotiate, but I'm hopeful that you'll see my skill at negotiating as something important that I can bring to the job." Basically, you've reframed your greedy, unfeminine need for money as a professional asset.

Justify Your Ask

Men don't have to couch their negotiations in somebody else's recommendation to be successful, but women often do. One possibility: "My manager suggested I talk to you . . ." A more powerful suggestion: framing the fact that you *are* negotiating as a professional asset ("I know you are expecting me to negotiate, since my job here is to *negotiate with clients . . .*").

Play to Your Boss's Ego

Ask for advice. You know how this goes: everybody loves to hear themselves talk . . . at least a little. It can help you to flip the script. You're making your boss invest emotionally in a good outcome for you.

Smile

Women shouldn't have to do this, but in the name of providing you with all the information: in an experiment in which women and men asked for raises using identical language, the Carnegie Mellon professor Linda Babcock found that the women were branded aggressive *unless* they gave a smile while they did it (or found another way to appear warm and friendly). In the grin-and-bear-it category: Try not to think of it as playing into a gender norm, but rather as smiling as you're thinking about your *fabulous* future.

Cash In Your Woman Card

It guarantees you a 21 percent discount! Just kidding. But talking up front about gender bias isn't necessarily a bad thing. I have one friend—a filmmaker—who walked into a salary negotiation and led with the following: "The research shows you're going to like me less after I negotiate. So I just wanted to get that out of the way before I do." Her delivery was friendly, almost nonchalant, and yet she was able to alert the other party to their own bias.

Do Not Retreat!

Women are more likely to compromise quickly—but don't do it. Don't automatically take the first offer on the table, and know that one round of discussion is sometimes not enough. I get it, you're dying to get this over with. But it's not actually a *negotiation* if you accept the only thing that's presented. Start by thanking everyone for the meeting, then asking to think about things overnight so you can plot your next move.

Practice

In front of the mirror, with a buddy, into your iPhone, whatever. You need to visualize victory and smooth talk the shit out of this negotiation.

WTF To Say:
A SCRIPT

SAY THIS

When establishing a number:

- "I've done some research, and it looks like the typical pay for somebody at my level is _____."

- "According to Salary.com [or source of your choosing], the standard rate is _____." (Makes it about market rates, not what you're worth. Walk into the meeting well researched.)

- "I typically get _____." (Useful because it provides a frame of reference.)

When making your case:

- "I feel great about what *we* accomplished this year." (Such a team player, aren't you!)

- "Based on [insert your best evidence for why you deserve it], I'd like to propose _____." (Still nice but to the point.)

- "The standard inflation rate is _____. Based on my performance over [period of time], I'd like to discuss an increase of _____." (Great, you've done your research.)

- If you feel you are doing the work of someone at a higher pay grade than you, make that your basis of negotiation. "I'm a second-year associate doing the work of a third year. I'd like to make my compensation commensurate with my output."

- Remember: Keep emotions out of it. Stay data driven and fact based.

When it starts to get heated:

- "I'm confident we can get to a place we both feel good about." (Collaborative, not confrontational.)

- "I think we are close." (Stays positive and keeps everyone engaged.)

DON'T SAY THIS

- "I can't afford to live in _____." (Your boss doesn't care.)

- "I have student loans." (Ditto.)

- "I'm getting married." (Nope.)

- "I'm trying to get pregnant." (Noooo!)

- "I've been working overtime." (We all work hard.)

- "This is what I want and I'll take nothing less." (Negotiation is about compromise.)

- "I need ____." (OK, but do you really *need* it? Try "I'd like" or "I propose.")

- "I'm sorry, I just want ____." (Do not—repeat: do not!—apologize for talking about money.)

- "I haven't had a raise/asked for anything since . . ." (Complaining will get you nowhere fast. If you really haven't asked for a raise in five years, mention this *after* you've made the case based on your work.)

- "But I'm doing the work of three people." (If that's true, then kudos, you're killin' it. But try framing this as an accomplishment instead of a complaint. You need a raise to be made "commensurate" with your workload.)

WHAT TO SAY IF THEY SAY . . .

"This is higher than what we've budgeted for this role."

- "I understand. I also believe I bring more to the table than the average candidate. [Insert how]."

"We don't think you're ready for that role."

- "Help me understand what I can do to *be* ready."

"We are thrilled to offer you (gut-punchingly lower amount than what you wanted)!"

- "Thank you so much. I'm really excited about the opportunity, *but*—
- What I'd need to feel comfortable accepting this role is ____."
- If you're able to match ____, I'd be eager to accept right now."
- "I know that the typical salary range for this role is ____, and I'm really looking to at least match that figure. Are you able to get to that level?"

After an initial round of negotiation: "Unfortunately, we can only go as high as—."

- Stay silent for long enough to take a breath. Then say, "I appreciate your flexibility in trying to make this work. I really want this job, so I'm hoping we can see what we can do to make both sides comfortable." (No, you're not offering a back rub, you're talking about nonmonetary items like stock, flexibility, benefits.) "How flexible are you with [insert benefit]?"
- "I understand, and I am eager to accept. I'd like to set up a timeline to revisit the terms again in ____ months. Is that something you're open to?" (Sets a concrete framework for a potential bump.)

After multiple rounds of negotiation: "I'm sorry, but we can only offer—."

- Ask them what they *can* do to make up the difference. (Again: stock, flexibility, benefits, something else.)
- "I understand. What if we set up a timeline to reassess in ____ months?"

HOW TO RESPOND

If the deal is good:

- Take it, and get to work. If an employer works to get you what you ask for, be appreciative and responsive. Sometimes, rapid decision making is needed.

If you aren't sure:

- "Thank you so much for the offer. I need a few days to think about it/weigh my options."

If it's *still* not good enough:

If it's a job you're in already:

- Take what's on the table and ask if you can reassess in six months.

- Take what's on the table and start looking for a new job immediately.

- Walk away from that soul-crushing job and never look back. Of course, you've got to first ask yourself if you can afford it—and if it's worth sucking it up a little bit longer until you find your next gig.

If it's a job you're negotiating *for:*

- Take what's on the table and ask if you can reassess in six months.

- Say no as a tactic. Keep in mind: this only works if you're *actually able/ willing to walk away.* But in a prolonged negotiation, it can be effective: sometimes it's the only thing that will make the person on the other end meet your demands.

- Actually walk away. And when writing a formal "I'm *out!*" show your disappointment but be gracious so the door stays open: "I appreciate your going to bat for me. Unfortunately, I'm unable to accept at that amount, but I hope that we can cross paths in the future. Thank you and please don't hesitate to call me if anything changes." As Beyoncé says: the best revenge is that paper.

- If they counteroffer with something good, take the job and get to work.

CONGRATS! YOU'VE NEGOTIATED. NOW HELP A LADY OUT.

After Jennifer Lawrence wrote an article about finding out how much less she was making than her male colleagues, Bradley Cooper announced that he'd start sharing his salary publicly—to highlight the pay gap. Here's what *you* can do:

Share What You Make

One journalist I know has started emailing other women she sees writing for the same outlets, offering to tell them how much she's getting paid—no reciprocity required. "If they're getting paid more, great, they don't have to tell me. If they're getting paid less, well then, they should know," she told me. "It's been a really useful tactic, both concretely and in terms of solidarity."

Create a Clearinghouse

A former engineer at Google created a spreadsheet where she and co-workers could share their salaries internally. Managers weren't happy about it, but people asked for and received raises based on the sheet's data. Other industries have tried versions of the same.

Talk About Your Salary!

How can you know what you're up against if you don't know what other people make?

Part Six

WWJD– WHAT WOULD JOSH DO?

CARRY YOURSELF with the CONFIDENCE of a Mediocre WHITE MAN

For many years, I had a friend, a work colleague, named Josh. Josh was the *master* of getting what he wanted—from smooth talking his way through a pitch he'd come up with on the spot, to keeping his cool when he had obviously fucked something up, to turning a job he hated in one department into a promotion in another (accompanied by a hefty raise). But my favorite Josh story involved his strategy for getting restaurant reservations by calling up an unassuming hostess and pretending to be his own assistant.

> "Yes, hello, I'm . . . David, calling from the office of Josh so-and-so—he'd like a table for three . . ."

We ate a lot of great meals thanks to this tactic—at places we'd never have been able to get into otherwise. Of course I would have *never* dared to call up those restaurants on my own.

Eventually, the women (and men) in our office started applying the following acronym to Josh, which we would then repeat to ourselves anytime we were stuck in a jam: WWJD? We observed Josh's every move, almost as a social experiment. Over time I realized that his approach to handling just about any workplace interaction was the utter and complete opposite of what I would do.

In meetings, he had a couple of tricks: First, he'd always sit at the table, and in the seat closest to the boss, arriving punctually or even early to guarantee his spot. Then, when everyone else was speaking loudly, trying to talk over one another, Josh would turn to face our boss and speak to him directly in a calm, low voice. The rest of us would watch dumbfounded, wondering what secret they were sharing. But this tactic helped to cement his power in the room.

☆ Sit on me ☆

Magazines are often centered on the political theater of the "ideas meeting," which is usually a gathering of all the top editors and writers, called by the person in charge. Each attendee is expected to bring story ideas, and each is expected to relay those ideas—really sales pitches for your own creativity and story-selecting prowess—to the rest of the room. It was a public competition. On most weeks, before ideas meetings, I'd border on a panic attack. I'd come up with twelve ideas then pare my list down to six, then decide that three were stupid, then obsess and labor over the other three, changing the angle on each story a half-dozen times.

What would Josh do? He'd ask anyone and everyone for their ideas—colleagues in other departments, outside freelance writers, bureau correspondents who wouldn't be in the meeting—then present them on behalf of the group. Next, he'd unapologetically campaign before the meeting in support for those ideas. Week after week, Josh would walk out with at least one assignment—for himself or somebody else—while I remained stuck in a spiral of frantic self-doubt, writing and crossing out those same three ideas.

All of this said, Josh was nothing if not a mensch. In his personal life, he loved hosting dinner parties and was a truly convivial and generous host. But at work Josh also didn't give a shit whether or not he was "liked." He'd never get on board with an idea or enterprise if there wasn't an obvious benefit for *him*. If there was a project he wanted to be a part of, or a new role he wanted to create, he didn't wait around to be asked—he took the initiative and just started doing.

I remember the first time I walked into a meeting where Josh and I were in the same room. *Who does this guy think he is?* I thought. And then I realized: I could learn from him. So I stopped getting mad and started taking notes.*

---

* You know who else took notes on men? Frances Perkins, Franklin D. Roosevelt's secretary of labor, and the first woman to serve in the U.S. cabinet. Early in her professional life, she took notes on male colleagues filed in a large red envelope labeled "Notes on the Male Mind."

WWJD?:
FAKE IT TILL YOU MAKE IT

It happens all the time—a guy pitching himself for a promotion he doesn't deserve, excusing himself from a shitty assignment, or looking so goddamn confident that everyone acts like he's the boss, when he's not even close. He's the intern vying for the full-time job who lists his current job title as "chief researcher," while his female counterpart vying for a similar job lists hers as "research intern." Both are *technically* true—if they are indeed the only (and therefore chief) researchers on staff. But our male candidate has what we might call *chutzpah* (not to be confused with utter bullshit). You can have it too.

FEMULATE HIM

🤜 Sound Sure Even If You're Not

Sure you might not be sure, but if you were Josh, you'd make sure you *sounded* sure. It's a secret Wall Street executive Carla Harris picked up early on in her career, after a mentor told her she was "too willing to show it" when she didn't know something. "When you appear unsure of a fact or an answer to a question, people start to doubt that you know what you are doing," the woman told her. What did Harris do? She simply changed her tone to *act* like she was sure. Confident half-truths will beat out hesitant truths almost every time.

🤜 Honest Overconfidence

Here's a stat I cite frequently: A woman will apply to an open job listing if and only if she thinks she meets all—that is, 100 freaking percent—of the requirements listed for that job. But a man? He'll apply for that job when he meets just *60 percent*. Perhaps it's the product of what one study dubbed "honest overconfidence"—in which men rate their performance as better than it actually is, while women tend to judge theirs as worse. Who's *actually* more qualified for the job? That's a great question. But it's safe to assume most hiring managers will never find out—because you haven't sent them your résumé.

👊 Be Your Own Hype Woman

Even Beyoncé had an alter ego—Sasha Fierce—to help her develop into a more confident stage performer. Most of us don't come out of the womb with rock-solid confidence. But acting confident, even if it's an act, will not only convince others that you're competent, it can lead to *actual* confidence. If you can't do it for yourself, try doing it for your alter *she*go—and hype the shit out of her.

WWJD?:
FAIL UP

It's a lesson that Silicon Valley has taken to heart: according to research by Shikhar Ghosh, a lecturer at Harvard, more than a third of venture-backed start-ups blow through their investors' money, and 70 to 80 percent do not deliver their return. But those start-up founders don't hide their failures; to the contrary, they flaunt them—blogging about them, gathering to talk about them at conferences like FailCon. You know what else most of these start-ups have in common, besides failure? They're run by . . . yep, men.

The female fear of failure begins early. Research by the psychologist Carol Dweck reveals that even in elementary school, girls tend to give up more quickly than boys—and more so the higher their IQ. That fear doesn't abate with age—particularly in male-dominated fields, where women's contributions tend to be judged more harshly. And when a woman does fail, she is more likely to believe it's personal—she sucked—while men view it as circumstantial (the business sucked).

It's not all bad. Women's fear of failure may prompt them to become better informed; they take the time to read up on their ideas so they can supply evidence. But then of course there's the feedback loop: People who fear failure are less likely to put forward ideas, to take intellectual risks, and more likely to quit. They tend to avoid new challenges in favor of sticking to what they're already good at. How can you learn if you don't try something new?

FEMULATE HIM

You're in Good Company

Executives called the pilot episode of *Seinfeld* "weak," claiming that no audience would want to watch the show again. Oprah was fired from her job as a reporter. *Harry Potter* was rejected on the first round, because publishers thought it was "too long" for a children's book. In short: the world is full of stories about successful people who failed on their first try, tried again, then succeeded on the next. Picasso had to produce more than twenty thousand pieces of art to make a few masterpieces that we remember—don't you think your odds are better?

Failure FOMO

In his book *Originals,* the business professor Adam Grant describes how there are two kinds of failures: those centered on action and those centered on inaction—or, failing by botching the thing you tried, or failing by not trying at all. Most people think, ahead of time, that it's the failed actions they'll regret the most: the anguish of a tanked business or the humiliation of the botched marriage proposal. But guess what? When people reflect on their biggest regrets, what they regret most are the *inactions*—or the failure to *try,* not the failure itself.

Learn From Your Mistake

"There is no school, no therapy session, no amount of money that will earn you the wisdom and strength learned by an epic fail mistake," says Rachel Simmons, a leadership coach at Smith College. She's right—research supports the fact that we indeed learn more from failure than success.

WWJD?:
KEEP COOL & JUST SAY NO

For a long time, I said yes to everything: assignments I didn't want, coffees with people I had no intention of (or remote interest in) working with; asks to "pick my brain" or "grab my quick feedback" even though my ideas and feedback are actually how I make a living. It's not just me though: women have a harder time than men saying no when they're asked to do stuff—and they're often met with surprise (and even hostility) when they do. There's a difference between saying no to a stranger and saying no to your boss, of course—so it's key to know your place. But there are also tactics to ensure that your own work doesn't suffer as a result.

YES Zombie

YES
YES YES
YES
YES

Responsible

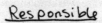

Sorry no!

FEMULATE HIM

👊 Rule of Reciprocity

For every stranger who's helped you, you may help a stranger in return. But take a moment to consider whether or not this is someone
you want to help, or need to help—and if not, is it possible to say no?
You don't need to be rude about it, but if it's a professional "ask," it's
appropriate to treat it as a business transaction. Ask yourself: What's
in it for me?

👊 Put the Work on Them

Does the person asking you want feedback? Make them send you a
proposal. Advice? Have them lay out exactly what they want evaluated. A recommendation? Ask for a bulleted list you can draw from.
Requests for assistance are often vague and unspecific, and they
almost always take more than "a quick moment." Don't waste time trying to figure out what the person wants—*require* that they explain it.

👊 Get a Stopwatch

One start-up founder told me that she considers anything that requires more than ten minutes of effort to be "consulting"—i.e., a paid
gig. Most of us aren't start-up founders, and I certainly have given
weeks of my life away if you add up the ten-minute increments. But
the point is setting boundaries ahead of time—for yourself and the
person who's asking.

WWJD?:
ASK FORGIVENESS, NOT PERMISSION

"Alexis" and "Nick" work at the same place, with jobs that require eighty-hour workweeks and tons of travel. Both of them have kids, and neither is happy about the lack of time they have to spend at home.

Alexis goes to her boss and requests her schedule be reduced—and the boss tries to accommodate. But Nick just *gives* himself a reduced schedule: working from home a couple of days a week, cultivating local clients to reduce his travel, making pacts with colleagues to cover for one another when they leave early. Both Alexis and Nick end their quarter with equal outcomes. But when it's time for their reviews, Nick's is stellar, while Alexis gets docked.

The names are made up but the scenario is real: from a study of a consulting firm by a professor at Boston University, who looked at the ways men and women responded to grueling, workaholic culture. What she found reaffirmed what many women will likely notice a thousand times over just a few years into the working world: that women tend to do the cautious, above-board thing and *ask* while men take the risks and *do*—assuming that all will be fine in the end.

FEMULATE HIM

🔖 **"Sorry," Not "Please"**

Most employees don't have nearly as much autonomy (or flexibility) as Alexis or Nick. If you're a shift employee you can't simply clock out without permission; if you're the only man of color in an all-white office, it's likely you aren't going to just slide by with the ease of Nick (who, based on the racial makeup of most consulting firms, we can likely assume was white). But women do tend to shy away from risk, particularly in male-dominated fields—often asking for *permission* instead of simply assuming that if things go wrong they can always say "I'm sorry." This scenario is big, but the philosophy behind it can be used on anything: Trying a new direction on a work task; leaving early for a doctor's appointment; sampling the candy in those bulk candy stores that are basically begging you to stick your hand in. Every job is different—and, as with all the advice here, consider your specific situation—but the point is to veer away from the female tendency to *ask* instead of take. Don't issue a press release about your plans just 'cause. Sometimes less information is more.

WWJD?:
IF AT FIRST YOU DON'T SUCCEED . . .

Here's what I do when I hear the word "no," or even no-adjacent ver-
biage: trudge back to my desk (or, these days, my couch), give up, sulk,
have a drink, cry, ruminate over what I did wrong, get mad at the other
person, get mad at myself, wonder what I could have done differently.
Here's what Josh would do when he heard the word "no": he'd calmly
walk back to his desk, regroup, perhaps grab a snack, then decide how
he was going to reframe the question to get a yes. Then he would go
back in and try again. This lesson is simple: pushback—whether it's
in the form of a challenge, a tepid response, negative feedback, or
even the actual word "no"—doesn't always *mean* no. So go back to the
drawing board—your desk, your couch, the handicapped stall in the
ladies' room where you do your best thinking—and do the following:

FEMULATE HIM

🤛 Say It like You Mean It

Was your idea delivered slump shouldered, in whisper voice, or with a self-defeating "I don't know if this is any good, but" preamble? Try again, this time like you mean it.

🤛 Reframe the Request

Whatever you've asked for or proposed, figure out the parts that drew the most criticism and either address them or restate them in a way your audience might like better.

🤛 Take Notes for Next Time

No might mean no. But what about the feedback you received—not the word "no," but the *reasons why*? Can you effectively weaponize them, using what you now know to get a yes on your next request? For example, in the best business-jargon I am capable of: "You mentioned we're short on budget, so I found a cost-effective way to . . ."

🤛 Don't Take It Personally

'Cause, yeah, we tend to (statistically speaking). In situations where a man and a woman each receive negative feedback, the woman's self-confidence and self-esteem drop to a much greater degree. Don't let it.

WWJD?:
DON'T HOPE, ASK

I was recently invited by an Internet company to curate an exhibit of female photographers in Los Angeles. It was not a paid gig, and I would have done it regardless, but I wanted something for my effort. Specifically, I wanted time in a hotel covered, so that I could kill time on the West Coast until a wedding I was supposed to attend. In my mind, this was a ridiculous thing to ask—because they *knew* it wasn't necessary. But I wrote an email asking for it anyway and ran it by a friend. "Ask for everything you want," she said. "What do you have to lose?" I did, and they didn't even flinch.

In her book *Women Don't Ask,* Linda Babcock describes two types of people: turnips, those who see little merit in asking for what they want (who perceive their environment as unchangeable) and oysters, those who see situations as adaptable and look for ways to improve them (they see the world as their oyster). Pretty sure you can guess which gender is likely to be which one. Babcock's book is about negotiation, but the premise applies to almost everything. Asking may not get you what you want. But you are *guaranteed* not to get it if you don't ask at all.

FEMULATE HIM

👊 Be an Oyster

Will you adapt/survive/continue to exist if this person says no? If the answer is yes, then ask. If the answer is no, then have a whiskey.

👊 Have a Counterplan for No

View your ask in shades of gray, not black and white. If they say no, is there a counteroffer to be made? Could you have *half* the deadline extension, or cover *half* the cost of the expense? Try asking—or backing down—in increments.

WWJD?:
ASSUME THE BEST

A friend tells a story about her husband: He works in a field where jobs are volatile, projects are always being deprioritized, bosses are changing their minds—and people's jobs suffer because of it. Something like this happens to her husband seemingly every six months, and each time, my friend Kyla, a social worker, *freaks the fuck out*. She starts looking for cheaper apartments and thinks about what will happen if they need to cut back. She cancels all upcoming vacations and picks up extra shifts at work. It's good to be prepared, but she goes full doomsday—all while her husband is seemingly nerves-free. Kyla is not an anomaly: women worry more than men. Surely Kyla's husband too has some sense of worry, but he also has the opposite attitude: that it will work out, that he's smart and capable, that if this job doesn't ultimately pan out he'll get an even *better* one. And if it doesn't go his way? He's surprised—while Kyla seems to have been preparing for the worst all along.

FEMULATE HIM

✊ Free Your Mind

What's going to happen is going to happen whether or not you worry. So cut back on a few unneeded expenses to be safe, but remind yourself that lying awake at night is not going to help solve the problem (and in fact it's likely to make you even more stressed). Think of all the *time* you'd save by not worrying. What world problems could you solve—or episodes of *Broad City* could you watch—with all this newly freed up mental real estate?

✊ The Rest Will Follow

Usually it does end up being fine. But what's key about Kyla's reaction is that she went straight to eviction. Maybe her husband struggles to regain his professional footing for a minute, but he's not envisioning them out in the street—he's secure in the knowledge that they'll be all right. Which is better for *his* mental health too. Nobody wants to be back on the job-hunt grind while simultaneously thinking that his *career is over*.

WWJD?:
GIRL, DO *YOU*

I have a joke among my journalism friends: that I've been outrunning the media grim reaper since I began my career. Where I go, layoffs, sales, and buyouts always seem to follow, from my hometown newspaper, the now-defunct *Seattle Post-Intelligencer,* to the *Village Voice* (a sale) to *Newsweek* (went out of, and then back into, print) to Tumblr (well, only *my* department was laid off). But by the time it was 2012, and I'd been forced into a freelance existence, I was over it. I was never taking a traditional journalism job again.

And so I didn't (at least not then). What I actually did, from my desk at Tumblr, where my computer would be confiscated by the end of the day, was to email Sheryl Sandberg. Yes, cold. I'd interviewed her once about negotiation and had written an article about her book. I knew she'd launched a nonprofit, I thought it sounded cool, and that they should probably hire somebody to help them create content. My email was brief, something to the effect of: "I got laid off. What are your plans for the foundation? Do you need an editor?"

She didn't, but she did have other jobs to fill—jobs I knew I didn't want. But she asked to meet, and I wasn't about to turn her down. So I proceeded to convince myself that I would convince *her* that there *was* a job to fill, and only *I* could do it. A half-dozen meetings and a twenty-five-page memo later, I had talked my way into a job—the job she said she wasn't hiring for.

FEMULATE HIM

Dancing on My Own

Perhaps it's a trickle-down effect of the start-up culture, but the ability to create one's own path is more common now than ever—and Josh would do this, I'm proud to say (!). He—no, she—would cold-email a professional idol and present her with a critique, boldly telling her what she needed to do differently, and making an argument for why *she'd* be the one to help her. When she had, she'd consider her offer and the requirement to move to San Francisco, which she had zero intention of doing, and present the case for why it made sense that she stay in New York. She would have no qualms about approaching a person she admired, who was doing something she wanted to be a part of, and she would assume that she had nothing to lose by asking. It appeared, then, that I had learned a little something from *Josh*.

What Kinda Shit Is This?
HOW TO SPOT A BULLSHITTER

Here's what business bros are great at: filling the air to *sound like* they know what they're talking about, even when they know about as much as the whiteboard they're gesturing in front of. But since the ban on bullshit isn't coming to America any time soon, a few crib notes for recognizing the practitioners of this dubious art.

BULLSHITTER: The Synergist

Says "synergy" and "pipeline" without an actual noun. Thinks "ideating" and "decisioning" are words and refuses to acknowledge otherwise.

SPIRIT ANIMAL: The Rabbit

 Much like the rabbit, the Synergist excretes a particular type of crap that is not particularly offensive when taken individually. But if you have to spend a day with this guy, these small pellets will amount to a huge, heaping pile of smelly crap.

BULLSHITTER: The Empty Wordsmith

Fills the room with long, vague phrases that mean nothing like, "Let's take a step back for a minute" or "Let's focus on the low-hanging fruit," then offers a generic platitude like, "We're all in this for the mission, right?"

SPIRIT ANIMAL: The Pigeon

 Like the pigeon, the Wordsmith's shit drops in unexpectedly in the middle of a meeting, leaving your mouth agape and your blazer covered in goo.

BULLSHITTER: The Grammarian

Loves the phrase "Let's unpack that statement" as an excuse to break said statement into its component parts, repeating what you've already said but in terms a child could understand. Also prone to chiming in at the end of a meeting to say, "So in summary . . .".

SPIRIT ANIMAL: The Mouse

 The mouse's bullshit is inoffensive and even sort of cute, if you take the repetition of your words as his way of complimenting your idea. But one too many rounds of "Let's unpack that" and you've likely got a full-fledged infestation on your hands.

BULLSHITTER: The Flatterer

Compliments the overall tone of the meeting without saying anything of substance. "I don't want to be too navel gazing but I feel like we're making great progress." He also enjoys agreeing with smart things other people have said, in hopes that his words will be associated with their wisdom.

SPIRIT ANIMAL: The Dog

 Like a puppy, this bullshitter smells a good idea and feels the need to piss on top of it, in order to add his own scent to the mix.

BULLSHITTER: The Disrupter

Uses the words "disrupt," "disruption," or "disruptive technology" because he thinks it makes him sound cool. Also frequently insists on "action items" and "key takeaways."

SPIRIT ANIMAL: The Cow

The cow can't help but put forth a horribly "disruptive" pile of heaping shit. The good news is he's impossible to miss for anyone with a sense of smell.

BULLSHITTER: The PowerPointer

Produces elaborate paper handouts or PowerPoint presentations. The more he dresses up the content—Venn diagrams, fancy fonts—the more he thinks it will "distract" from the lack of substance.

SPIRIT ANIMAL: The Sloth

The sloth takes days to coordinate its weekly poop, traveling a rough terrain of foliage, branches, and tree trunk in order to finally get the job done (at the bottom of its tree). It's a lot of effort put into an act that leaves the sloth vulnerable to predators.

BULLSHITTER: The Closer

Arrives to the meeting completely unprepared, waits until it's almost over, then chimes in to question the reason for having the meeting in the first place. "Wait, guys, can I just ask what we're trying to do here?"

SPIRIT ANIMAL: The Cat

Sneaky, undetectable, and likely to be hiding in a dark corner under a whiteboard somewhere—you won't see this bullshit coming until its stench suddenly hits you.

How To Have a D*ck Without Being One:

A PENILE SERVICE ANNOUNCEMENT (PSA)

Dear Male Comrades, Buddies, Guys, Pals, Etc.:

Please allow me to womansplain for a moment. You, men, are crucial to this battle. We need you on our team! This (life) is a co-ed sport. For the time being, you're half the population, the leaders of our companies, our politicians and executives, the fathers of our children, our partners and friends—and, most importantly, we cannot bring down the patriarchy without you, the patriarchy. Remember when you voted to let us vote? Same idea.

I know it's sort of weird, asking you to bring down the patriarchy, when the patriarchy *is* The Man, and you are men. It's like asking Big Tobacco to advertise against smoking, or asking Matthew McConaughey to put a shirt on. But winning this battle doesn't mean you lose. This isn't a zero sum game. Until the robots take over, you need us, and we need you to keep this whole life thing going.

Also: liberating *us* means liberating *you:* making your companies more profitable and cooperative, us earning more money so that you don't have to, raising kids who grow up to be healthier and more confident because they have working mothers and engaged fathers, and helping you make smart decisions at work. That and you get to hang out with us a lot, and we smell really good, usually like flowers, really poisonous flowers.

We know it can be scary to be a man these days. We'd be afraid of mansplaining too. But this is where the FFC can help. There is *tons* of easy stuff that guys can do on a daily basis to ensure they are keeping their D in check—and, more so, to be among ladies' best and most important advocates. Behold: a handy list to guide you. Tear it out and keep it in a safe spot.

GIVE US CRED

Women's ideas are less likely to be correctly attributed to them—and often because somebody else (a man) is repeating them more loudly. You guys could quiet down. But you could also give us credit, and it will make us *and* you look better in the process (us smart, you like the generous team player you are, right?). Our ideas aren't memes you can just repost, and it is annoying having to point it out (and we come off like buzzkills when we do). So do us a favor and hand over the credit when we deserve it.

CHECK YO' SPREAD

We're sick of hearing about manspreading too—and, we get it, it looks really comfortable—but men really do take up more space: a ten-to fifteen-degree angle more. We get it, there's more down there, but

Gore Vidal crossed his legs, so you can too. So, scoot your chair four inches away, adjust whatever needs adjusting, and please, close your legs. People have been telling us to do it for years.

INTERRUPT A MANTERRUPTER

Women are interrupted at twice the rate of men. So you can stop interrupting, but even better—because you're reading this book and so obviously must not interrupt—you can be a Manterrupter Interrupter, interjecting manterruptions on behalf of your female colleagues. It's as easy as "Hey, can you let her finish?" Maybe come up with a signal for your male colleagues when they're manterrupting, like in baseball. Now it's fun, like sports. You guys like sports. Guess what, so do women.

LET US TALK

Forget everything you've heard about "chatty" women—it's not true, that's just us talking, just like you, but actually less. I promise: when it comes to work, you really do talk more than we do—and often you have no idea how *much* more. So, please: try to keep your mouth shut long enough to let us finish. Then keep it shut a little while longer, we might have something else to say.

NOD WHEN WE SAY SMART THINGS

Particularly in a crowd, to show that you agree. (Yup, a man's validation still counts for more.) You can do this in email threads, too, by replying all with some form of "YES" or "agree." Emojis work too. I personally like the praise hands, claps, or even a bunch of 100s.

WE'LL TAKE A CAPPUCCINO

Thanks. If you could grab us one while you're picking up your *own* coffee on your way to work (milk alternative, please)—so you won't feel inclined to ask your female coworker to grab you one—that would be great. Also great is offering to take the notes in meetings. This type of grunt work more frequently falls to women—and while nobody *really* wants to take the notes, you guys benefit when you do (bosses think you're great, you get promotions and raises, yadda yadda). Male privilege is the best, right?

INVITE US TO MEETINGS

And, like, as many of us as you can round up. We are more likely to speak up if there are more women around, and we have really good ideas. We also smell good, and take up less room (manspreading again).

WATCH YOUR WORDS

Don't call us nags, or crazy, bossy, or aggressive. It hurts our feelings, but it's also fucked up: we are nags and bossy for exhibiting the same behavior you do, except that when you do it you're simply "reminding" or being "stern." Sometimes even when you're being "redundant" or "a dick." While we're at it, please refrain from infantilizing language too: we're not your "kiddo" or your "sweetie," and especially not "sugar." We may be cute, but our ideas are killer, and sometimes, *gasp*, better.

PRACTICE VAGFFIRMATIVE ACTION

Yep you read that right: That means if you have the power to hire—or even pass along a résumé—*do not* do so until you have an equal number of female candidates. Even better if you *only* pass on female resumes. Other ways you can help: If you turn down a job, think about which *women* you could recommend for it. Find at least one woman you can mentor. Find out who makes what on your team—and if the women are making less, fix it (or at least report it to somebody who can).

DO THE DISHES

If you can kill it in the bedroom, chances are you can kill it in the kitchen, too—and studies have shown that men who help out more with the chores have more sex with their wives (really!). We know, gender roles run deep, which is why women in hetero relationships still end up doing the vast majority of the domestic work despite being the breadwinners in two-thirds of American homes, leaving them burned out, resentful, and, nope, not really in the mood. But it doesn't have to be this way—and, in fact, we might want to borrow a page from our LGBTQ sisters and brothers (or those who identify as neither): research shows they split chores, decisions, and finances more evenly. Relationships are all about compromise, right? So think of it this way: I'll strip down, and you put my clothes in the laundry.

WEAR THE BABY BJORN

Being an engaged dad is good for all kids—it helps them cognitively, emotionally, socially, and, ultimately, economically. If you're the dad of a daughter, your job is particularly important, affecting her self-esteem, her autonomy, and her aspirations (according to one study, out of the University of British Columbia, daughters who see their dads doing chores are less likely to limit their career aspirations to stereotypically female industries, like teaching or nursing). But you can't just talk the talk, you have to actually walk it. We promise, it'll pay off for you, too! Working dads who spend more time with their kids are happier in their jobs. They're also more patient, empathetic, and flexible—and at least one study claims it might just help them live longer.

TAKE TIME OFF

If your company offers a paternity leave policy, set a precedent and take it. If *every* parent took time off to care for their kids, balancing work and family wouldn't be a "women's" problem. It's very European, and we both know you fancy yourself well traveled.

SUPPORT COMPANIES THAT SUPPORT WOMEN

Companies with more women in leadership are more successful: more collaborative, more profitable, and more inclusive, and having more women in power may actually encourage women to bring their ideas forward. They also smell better. (Did we mention that?) So if you're going to bother buying Toms shoes, "sustainable" hair gel, or that "fair trade" coffee, why not apply the same idealism to companies that support women? I bet you come in way more contact with disenfranchised women than barefoot children.

FFC FOREVER

CONCLUSION

Sisters in Arms

"Whatever you choose, however many roads you travel, I hope that you choose not to be a lady. I hope you will find some way to break the rules and make a little trouble out there."

—Nora Ephron

There was a brief period in 2014 when a few of us in the Fight Club seemed to hit rock bottom at once. I had gotten dumped after an eight-year relationship, gone freelance, and was now working out of my apartment, a.k.a my bed. When I was not too depressed to get out of said bed, I was struggling to juggle four different jobs, and I had broken out with an unexplained stress rash.

There was one particular afternoon when I was coaxed out of my house by some Fight Club members for a sanity check. Three of us met at a café in the East Village, and after we ordered, each proceeded to take out her respective prescription bottle (antidepressants; probiotics; tic tacs), swallow them with coffee, and then spend ten minutes talking about our bowel movements. We all had stress-induced IBS.

It was me, Amanda, and Asie. Amanda, a comedy writer, had—after months of searching for a new job while she toiled in a shitty one—quit without another one lined up. She was "free," finally—but also not living for "free," and so she was desperate for any work we could send her way. Asie, a set makeup artist and stylist, was four months pregnant and struggling to muster that enthusiastic "soooo excited, the gift of *motherhood*!" grin you're apparently supposed to have when people congratulate you. She was happy, but she was also terrified of what a baby meant for her career. Already she was too nauseated to work. She was extrasensitive to smells—and a makeup artist has to be all up in everybody's face.

We bought Amanda lunch, and Amanda fanned Asie with a menu when she thought she might vomit all over our table. Asie told me I needed to wash my hair. And then we burst out laughing.

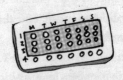

This was the beauty of the Fight Club, in a sense: that each of us, at a certain point, had been downtrodden, unemployed, directionless, broke, unshowered, or feeling terrible. And just as we could rely on one another for support when things were good, we could commiserate when things were bad. Many in the group were successful—but nobody is successful *all the time.* "That was what made it so good: we were all fucking *in it,*" said Amanda. "We could celebrate the glories— but we could talk about the shit, too."

And was there a lot of shit. We were gaining our feet professionally, which meant that sometimes doors would open and others would close—often in our faces. We had brought in some members because they were lost or floundering. Others had joined because they were unemployed. And then there was the life shit that gets thrown into the mix: breakups, moves, sick parents, babies, or the terror that we'd somehow "chosen" our career at the expense of all those other things.

But there were also a lot of victories. Negotiating raises. Boasting on one another's behalf. Sharing job listings, passing on one another's résumés, sharing whatever perks—tickets to a conference, a movie, or a lecture—came along with our respective jobs. There were times we heard ourselves complain so many times that we suddenly started to focus, to commit, or, conversely, to realize that the thing we were complaining about was actually doable—even conquerable—with the right support. Sometimes we just needed to get it out, to vent, to laugh, and to go back to work a little lighter the next day.

Nearing our sixth anniversary, we met at my house one evening and ate a cake. Like we do at most gatherings, we went around the group and each gave a job update—along with one thing we were proud to have accomplished. One member had sold a television show and had hired another member to direct it. Another had just accepted a new job as a producer—a job for which one Fight Club member edited her application package and another got it to the right person. There was a trivia writer who was working at *Who Wants to Be a Millionaire*. She hated the job but had turned it into a game of sorts: for every sexist remark she heard in the office, she would vow to get one more piece of feminist trivia onto the show. The last person to speak was a new face. She'd just quit her job at a marketing firm and decided to try to make it as a writer full-time—thanks to the money she'd won on (wait for it) *Who Wants to Be a Millionaire*.

Nora Ephron once said that if you slip on a banana peel you are the joke. But if you *tell* everyone you slipped on a banana peel—well, then it's your laugh. In a way, the Fight Club flipped the banana peel metaphor: no longer were we slipping; we were gliding, carried by a wave of support and reassurance. The meetings were the structure—but the friendships and emails and field trips and laughs were what kept us going, biding our time until things got better, without being tempted to do anything rash (or, at least, get a rash).

"That was the air in our lungs," explained Asie, now with a ten-month-old daughter, the Fight Club's youngest member. "It was going to a bar and laughing. Texting when sick or poor or disappointed. Or paying for someone's lunch, because she quit her miserable sexist job.

"It was knowing we were not alone."

Join the

FEMINIST FIGHT CLUB!

WHERE TO MEET

A 1969 handbook, *How to Start a Consciousness-Raising Group,* ordered the following: "Hold your first meeting in a place where you will not be disturbed by husbands, boyfriends, children, or visitors." The FFC is not quite so particular. A few suggestions: a dorm room, an apartment, a coffee shop, the library, a park, the dressing room of a Forever 21, the girls' locker room at the gym, the back of a taxi, a classroom, Skype.

WHAT TO TALK ABOUT

- Start with a question: Why did you come to a Feminist Fight Club? Where do you want to be in five years? What's your biggest office pet peeve?

- Talk about your job goals—and ask one another how you can help achieve them.

- Share a story. Explain the last time you were proud at work, and why.

- Analyze. Try out an FFC fight move and keep detailed notes on how it worked. Report back.

THINGS TO DO

Manless Dinners

A dinner of all ladies from which many a revolution has emerged. (From a 1916 *New York Times* headline: "At Manless Dinner, Women Speak of the Achievements of Their Sex.") Host one with your lady friends.

Lady Fridays

Flip the script and do stereotypically masculine things with your lady friends. Suggestions: poker night, Guitar Hero jam sesh, video games, beer pong.

Make a Zine!

A cheap, badass form of print that requires nothing but a pen, a copy machine, and paper. Sample topics: Fight Clubs, Nicki Minaj, bacon, favorite plants, dogs, first kisses, fandom, girl crushes.

Interview a Female Member of Your Family

What have you never asked? You might be surprised what you learn.

Vision Boarding

Devote a night with your Fight Club to "visioning" your goals for the next year. These can be professional, personal, or something else. Just make them *specific* so you can track your progress. Now sit around on the floor, pretend you're back in your high school bedroom collaging, and create a masterpiece that conveys those goals. Necessary supplies: old magazines, construction paper, tape, scissors, glitter, more glitter.

Plan a Zap!

That's 1960s-speak for theatrical protests: you know, dressing up as witches and putting a "hex" on creepy male officeworkers; organizing an "ogle-in" to protest street harassment (both real actions carried out by groups of women). What do you feel passionately about? What irks you the most at your office, or your campus? Create a protest around it. Ideas: Make stickers that say "FFC IS WATCHING" and place them over the mouths of sexist ads you see on the subway. Organize the women in your office to wear your bulkiest winter gear for a day—to protest how goddamn cold the air conditioning is.

Assignment:
WRITE A LETTER TO A GALPAL

Long before the modern workplace, before phones or trashy TV, even before *pants* for women, there were girlfriends. Girlfriends with a bond so close that, as far back as the sixteenth century, it was understood that while a woman could share the same soul with her best girlfriend, she could rarely—if ever—share one with her husband.

Friendships weren't just a way of getting through the monotony of those old days—they were often political pacts too. The path to women's voting rights was laid in part by the lasting friendship between Susan B. Anthony and Elizabeth Cady Stanton.* It was a "manless dinner" thrown by the activist Jane Hunt—for her friend Lucretia Mott—that resulted in the first-ever women's rights convention, at Seneca Falls, in 1848. Even Eleanor Roosevelt's political rise occurred in part because of the central role that her friends played in her life.

And all of these girlfriends, do you want to know how they communicated? They communicated via *letters*. Yes, letters, like you'd send a pen pal, with the key word being "pen": actual ink pen. These letters conveyed frustrations with their roles at the time; they led to organizing strikes and protests; they expressed deep affection for one another. They were often signed: "Thine in the bonds of sisterhood."

Kind of cool, right?

So here's your FFC homework: Write a letter to a galpal and tell her how much she means to you.

---

* Who, for what it's worth, had the word "obey" omitted from her marriage vows when she wed her husband, Henry Brewster Stanton.

DEAR GIRLFRIEND,

DON'T FORGET

YOU DON'T HAVE TO SMILE

MOOD

LOVE,

FUCK DIAMONDS, YOU ARE MY BEST FRIEND

A Feminist Cocktail List

(Consensual) Sex on the Beach

Ask your lady friend
what she wants in her
drink. Add peach schnapps.
Give it to her.

The Not-So-Old-Fashioned

Order an Old Fashioned.
Then talk about how great
it is to have a job, live in
your _own_ apartment, and
not be married.

The Prince Charming

Get so drunk with
your lady friends
you lose a shoe.

The UTI

Vodka.
Cranberry.
Repeat!

The Suffragist

Have your gal pals vote
on what to drink.
Get a pitcher of it.

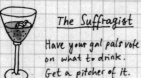

The Long Island Iced Tease

Let somebody buy you
a Long Island Iced Tea.
Don't go home with them.

Lady Beer

Beer.
It was invented
by women

1. WORK IT - MISSY ELLIOT 2. CONTROL - JANET JACKSON 3. NONE OF YOUR BUSINESS - SALT-N-PEPA 4. CRAZY ON YOU - HEART 5. INDESTRUCTIBLE - ROBYN 6. ***FLAWLESS - BEYONCE

7. REBEL GIRL - BIKINI KILL

FEMINIST FIGHT CLUB
THE MIX TAPE

8. FEELING MYSELF - NICKI MINAJ

9. NO SCRUBS - TLC 10. STAND BACK - STEVIE NICKS 11. BITCH BETTER HAVE MY MONEY - RIHANNA

12. CHERRY BOMB - THE RUNAWAYS TKO - LE TIGRE 13. CAN'T HOLD US DOWN - CRISTINA AGUILERA & LIL' KIM 15. Q.U.E.E.N. - JANELLE MONAE & ERYKAH BADU 16. WHIP MY HAIR - WILLOW

17. TECH BRO - CHILDBIRTH 18. GIRLS! GIRLS! GIRLS! - LIZ PHAIR 19. DOO WOP (THAT THING) - LAURYN HILL

Rebel Girls:
FFCs THROUGH HISTORY

ALPHA SUFFRAGE CLUB

More than seventy years before Rosa Parks would refuse to give up her seat, it was the founder of this black suffrage group, Ida B. Wells, who sued the Memphis and Charleston Railroad after she was ordered out of the first-class ladies car. Twenty-nine years later, she would arrive in Washington to participate in the 1913 suffrage parade and be asked to march in the back—at which Wells promptly took her place at the front of the line.

BIBLE REVISION COMMITTEE

 These twenty-six women, under the leadership of Elizabeth Cady Stanton, gathered in the late 1800s to write *The Woman's Bible*—which challenged the traditional position of religious orthodoxy that woman should be subservient to man.

BRUJAS

Named after the Spanish for "witch," this Latina skate crew from the Bronx embodies barrio girl pride—encouraging women of color to participate in skate culture. Taking their name from the 1980s punk cult film *Skate Witches*—about a group of teenage female skater punks who terrorize boy skaters—the Brujas have been skating together since they were twelve years old. "Brujas is not a counterpart to any male gang," the women say. "It's our own gang."

BURNED OUT BUSINESSWOMEN'S ASSOCIATION (BOBWA)

This club's common bond? Exhaustion. Dubbing themselves "BOB-WAnians," this group was founded in 1994 by a Kansas City mother and full-time executive, Marcia Hines, who found herself "just really, really tired all the time."

CELL 16

"Women! Come and join us if you need to breathe." That was the newspaper ad for women to join this Boston group, which would help set up street patrols around the city in places where women were being raped. In 1969, Cell 16 strode onto the stage of the first-ever women's congress, in New York City, and cut off their long hair—because, as they put it, long hair "belongs" to men.

CHULITA VINYL CLUB

 This all-vinyl, all-female DJ collective, based in south Texas, mixes rock, soul, and punk with rare, Chicano-flavored records—and aims to turn the male-dominated DJ culture on its head.

COMBAHEE RIVER COLLECTIVE

Named for the Combahee River in South Carolina, where Harriet Tubman freed 750 slaves, this group of black lesbian feminists began meeting in Boston in the 1970s to defy the triple threat of being black, lesbian, *and* female. Formed as an offshoot of the National Black Feminist Organization, they sponsored retreats along the East Coast, funded local battered women's shelters, and issued a statement that critiqued the racism of the mainstream women's movement.

THE FEMINISTS

This group had a leaderless structure, advocated for reparations for women, and mandated that no more than 30 percent of members could be married (eventually, they banned all women living with men from their ranks). In 1969, the women picketed the New York City Marriage Bureau, accusing the city of "fraud with malicious intent."

FEMINIST KARATE UNION

This Seattle self-defense center was formed as a response to Ted Bundy, the serial killer who preyed on young women in Washington and Oregon in the 1970s. The Union remains a full-time karate school for women and children, taught by women.

THE FURIES

This collective of "lesbians in revolt" lived together in the early 1970s, sharing clothes, household duties, and starting a school to teach auto and home repair so they wouldn't have to rely on men. The Furies were one of many lesbian separatist clubs of the era, who formed "womyn's lands," gave themselves names like CLIT Collective and the Van Dykes, and saw lesbianism "not a matter of sexual preference, but rather one of political choice."

GRAY PANTHERS

Proving that women don't just evaporate after the age of fifty (!), this elder-rights group was founded by the activist Maggie Kuhn after her forced retirement from the Presbyterian Church. Still active today, the Gray Panthers contend that "old people and women constitute America's biggest untapped and undervalued human energy source."

GUERRILLA GIRLS

This anonymous group of artists has spent three decades storming the art world, calling attention to sexism, racism, and wage inequity with guerrilla-style street art—all while wearing gorilla masks. One of their posters, featuring a naked woman with a gorilla head, asks: "Do women have to be naked to get into the Met Museum?"

JANE COLLECTIVE

"Jane" was the code name for this underground abortion group, which helped more than eleven thousand women get safe and illegal procedures before the *Roe v. Wade* decision. They operated by word of mouth, transporting women by car to two apartments that they used as their clinic, and ultimately learning how to conduct abortions themselves.

LADY CYCLISTS ASSOCIATION

As the suffragist Susan B. Anthony told journalist Nellie Bly in 1896, bicycling "has done more to emancipate women than anything else in the world." Bicycles allowed women new mobility, independence, and the ability to explore beyond their neighborhoods.

THE LESBIAN AVENGERS

Their motto playfully proclaimed "we recruit," and recruit this group did. Formed in the 1990s to bring attention to lesbian causes, the Lesbian Avengers spent Valentine's Day handing out chocolate kisses in Grand Central Station that read, "You've just been kissed by a lesbian." In Bryant Park, they unveiled a papier-mâché sculpture of Alice B. Toklas embracing her lover, Gertrude Stein. The Avengers also ate fire, which would become their dramatic trademark—first practiced as an homage to an Oregon gay man and lesbian woman who were burned to death after a Molotov cocktail was thrown into the apartment they shared.

LIBERATION SCHOOL FOR WOMEN

They taught women to tell a distributor from a carburetor; the clitoris from the vulva; and how to get a divorce without a lawyer. Formed in Chicago in the 1970s, this group was made up of women who were cashiers, secretaries, teachers, nurses, students, and homemakers, most with little or no college education.

LOWELL MILL GIRLS

Half a century before the better-known movements for workers' rights, the women of the Lowell, Massachusetts, textile mills went on strike to protest hellish labor conditions—creating the first union of working women in American history.

LUCY STONE LEAGUE

 Named for the early feminist crusader Lucy Stone—the first woman to keep her maiden name—this club was founded in 1921 to protect a woman's right to her surname. "Lucy Stoners," as the women were known, were instrumental in strengthening the right of women to own property and sign legal documents in their own names.

MILITANT HOUSEWIVES

These Depression-era women staged boycotts and lobbied for price controls on food and rent across the country. In Cleveland, black women hung wet laundry over utility lines to protest electricity shutoffs. In Chicago, Polish women stormed a meat warehouse and set fire to thousands of pounds of meat to show that raised prices were not the result of "shortages." In New York, Jewish women resisted eviction by barricading themselves inside their homes, brandishing scalding kettles of water they threatened to toss onto anybody who tried to move their furniture.

MORAL REFORM SOCIETY

It was a group of wives who banded together to form this group, lobbying against brothels by standing outside, with clipboards, and recording the names of the married men who went in. The group founded halfway houses for reformed prostitutes, lobbied for women's education and employment, and, in 1848, helped get the first abduction and anti-rape laws passed in New York State.

NATIONAL ASSOCIATION OF COLORED WOMEN

Under the motto "Lifting as We Climb," this group's founding members included some of the most renowned educators, abolitionists, and activists of our time—including Harriet Tubman, Frances E. W. Harper, and Ida B. Wells. Founded in Washington, D.C., in 1896, the group focused on assisting impoverished women through job training, advocating for wage equality, education, and housing, as well as drawing attention to lynching, prison conditions, and segregation.

THE NEWSGIRLS

This all-female, trans-inclusive boxing club in downtown Toronto earned six medals at the Canadian boxing nationals in 2010. In addition to regular boxing classes and Friday night "GirlFights," the club has movie nights, a sewing group, and participates in fund-raisers for local rape crisis and women's shelters.

NEW YORK RADICAL WOMEN

Founded as a more radical alternative to mainstream women's orgs like the National Organization for Women, this group would gain notoriety for its 1968 Miss America protest in Atlantic City—in which they unveiled a giant "WOMEN'S LIBERATION" banner inside the pageant and threw bras, girdles, curlers, and false eyelashes into a "Freedom Trash Can." (No, they never actually burned bras.)

NUNS ON THE BUS

This group of Roman Catholic nuns formed in 2012, in response to the Vatican claim that American nuns were promoting "radical feminist themes incompatible with the Catholic faith." These nuns went on the road—visiting homeless shelters, food pantries, and other sites across nine states to highlight the value of their community service work.

OUR BODIES, OURSELVES

They published the first book to teach women about masturbation, birth control, and—yes—the clitoris (spelled out as *klit-o-ris*), distributed as a photocopied pamphlet in Boston for seventy-five cents. The authors were twelve women, none of them medical experts, who believed, rightly, that with better knowledge, women would be better equipped to deal with their own health.

OVARIAN PSYCOS BICYCLE BRIGADE

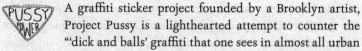 With "ovaries so big we don't need balls," this all-woman, mostly Latina bike gang formed in 2011 Los Angeles—a response to the city's predominantly male bike culture. Made up of nonprofit workers and community activists, the group holds "womyn's jiu jitsu" events, full moon bike rides, and an annual ride called Clitoral Mass.

PROJECT PUSSY

A graffiti sticker project founded by a Brooklyn artist, Project Pussy is a lighthearted attempt to counter the "'dick and balls' graffiti that one sees in almost all urban contexts." To do that, members draw colorful vaginas and stick them onto public property around New York City.

RATIONAL DRESS SOCIETY

The society believed that no woman should have to wear more than seven pounds of underwear. Recognizing the restrictive nature of Victorian-era women's clothes—whalebone corsets, petticoats, bustles, and heavy skirts—this group advocated for a style of dress based on "health, comfort and beauty" that would allow women to get around more easily.

RIOT GRRRL

Riot Grrrl roared into the spotlight in the early 1990s out of dreary Olympia, Washington—producing politically charged punk that combined activism and art. Forged out of a meeting of friends who decided they wanted to start a "girl riot," the women gave rise to bands like Bikini Kill and Sleater-Kinney, addressing rape and violence in their songs, publishing zines, popularizing "girl power," and inspiring thousands of riot grrrls around the country. Supporting other women was always part of Riot Grrrl's message: at Bikini Kill concerts, women got to stand in the front.

THE RED BRIGADE

Working to shatter the taboo of menstruation, this group of women covered themselves in red paint and marched through the Michigan Womyn's Music festival in 2001, with slogans that included "Join the Red Revolution!" and "Get Corporations Out of Our Cunts." They also published a zine called *Red Alert*.

REDSTOCKINGS

The Redstockings told women to "bitch sisters, bitch." Known for "speakouts"—women speaking publicly about their abortions—and "zap" protest actions, the group's name represented the union of two traditions: the "bluestocking" label disparagingly pinned on women of earlier centuries and "red" for revolution.

SATURDAY MORNING GIRLS

Founded by a Boston woman in 1871—after her daughter asked why there were no clubs for girls—this group offered an alternative to the sewing clubs and debutante balls that defined the lives of middle- and upper-class women at the time. They met on Saturday mornings to discuss math and science, learning to draft a constitution, adopt by-laws, and elect officers.

S.C.U.M.

A 1967 manifesto by a New York City writer name Valerie Solanas, *S.C.U.M.* parodied man as an "incomplete female" who was deficient due to the Y chromosome causing him to be emotionally stunted, egocentric, and lacking empathy. It was distributed on two thousand mimeographed copies throughout the village, charging women one dollar and men two dollars.

SHAMELESS HUSSY

This all-female publishing house was formed in 1969, a time when 94 percent of the books printed in the United States were written by men. Over the course of twenty years, many female writers would find their voice here, including the group's founder, who published the first book of overt lesbian love poems in America. "Shameless hussy" was a phrase her mother had used for women she didn't approve of.

SOJOURNER TRUTH DISCIPLES

Named for the fiery abolitionist Sojourner Truth, a former slave, this 1960s club, made up of ex-inmates in Philadelphia, was devoted to improving the conditions of women in prison.

THE SUFFRAGISTS

They were the original squad: parading and picketing, lighting bonfires, having their fingers broken by police, and being subjected to psychiatric torment in an attempt to curb their "antisocial behaviors." To them we owe the Nineteenth Amendment, which granted women the right to vote.

THAT TAKES OVARIES!

It began as an offhand remark—"Well, that takes ovaries!"—that developed into a theater troupe that tells the stories of brazen acts by women. Having ovaries, say the group's founders, isn't just about possessing certain organs, but possessing "a certain Attitude (with a capital A)."

THIRD WORLD WOMEN'S ALLIANCE

This 1970s group published the *Black Women's Manifesto,* cosigned by Eleanor Holmes Norton and Frances M. Beal, whose famous 1969 essay, "Double Jeopardy: To Be Black and Female," is considered one of the defining texts of that era. The manifest declared: "The black woman is demanding a new set of female definitions and a recognition of herself as a citizen, companion and confidant, not a matriarchal villain or a step stool or baby-maker."

TRUTH SQUADS

These groups of nine or ten women, popular in New York City in the 1960s, would burst in unannounced on somebody's husband and confront him with a list of grievances.

WAC

Men were not welcome in WAC—but bad attitudes were. A group forged in response to the sexist treatment of Anita Hill, WAC was nonhierarchical and performance driven, using drums and dildo squirt guns to stage colorful demonstrations they called "WAC attacks."

WASPS

In 1942, as America reeled from the attack on Pearl Harbor, qualified male pilots were in high demand and short supply—so a group of women stepped in. Known as WASPs, or Women Airforce Service Pilots, these women formed the country's first female squadron. Though they were never recognized as members of the U.S. military, these women were vital to the war effort.

THE WEENIE WACKERS

"A for a lay" it was called: an unofficial policy in which male college professors would offer grades for sexual acts. It was common in the 1960s, on campuses like Sacramento State, where one group of women had had enough. On Halloween, they dressed up as witches, strapped dildos and bras on their heads, and one by one went to the offices of known perpetrators to put a hex on them. "Shame on you!" the women would declare, as horrified office administrators stood by. One of the men wasn't in his office—so they went by his house and spray-painted "A pig lives here" for all to see.

WIMMEN'S COMIX COLLECTIVE

With titles such as *Tits & Clits* and *Dynamite Damsels,* this group of female comic book artists got together in the 1970s to combat sexism in the underground comics scene. The collective operated until 1992, making it the longest-lasting all-woman comic book anthology in history.

WOMEN'S LIBERATION ROCK BAND

This real (yes real) band formed in New Haven and Chicago in the 1970s and released an album of songs that included "Ain't Gonna Marry," "Dear Government," and "So Fine."

THE WOMEN'S SALOON

Its walls were decorated with female art, there was a ban on diet drinks, and waitresses were not required to smile or be "perky." Founded in Los Angeles in 1974, the saloon allowed women who couldn't afford drinks to work off their debt by washing dishes.

WOMEN OF ALL RED NATIONS

WARN was the best-known Native American women's organization of the 1970s, made up of women from more than thirty tribes. They were instrumental in the campaign to halt the government-imposed surgical sterilization of Native American women.

WOMEN'S GRAPHICS COLLECTIVE

With posters that declared "WOMEN WORKING UNITE!" and "Women Are Not Chicks," this group was responsible for much of the visual iconography of the women's movement. They operated in Chicago, on a shoestring budget, and could be reached by mail—though, as they once noted, they were "sick of getting letters addressed 'Dear Sir.'"

W.I.T.C.H.

Members of the Women's International Terrorist Conspiracy from Hell dressed as witches and appeared on the floor of the New York Stock Exchange to ogle men. Proclaiming witches to be the original female rebels—the group devoted itself to guerrilla theater called "zaps."

W.O.W.

Representing more than 800,000 clerical workers, the World Organization of Workers fought to end race, sex, and age discrimination, filing complaints against employment agencies. In 1979, the group published a leaflet stating, "The happiest day of my life was when I discovered my clitoris."

A Space for

BATTLE NOTES

DATE OF BATTLE

OPPONENT

LOCATION

SPECIFICS

FIGHT MANEUVER USED

_____

_____

_____

DID IT WORK?

_____

_____

_____

NOTES FOR NEXT TIME

_____

_____

_____

_____

_____

_____

_____

_____

_____

_____

_____

_____

_____

_____

ACKNOWLEDGMENTS

This book would not exist without the unwavering support of a vast collective of women and men.

First and foremost, Amanda McCall, whose humor and insight and edits and puns this book would truly not exist (or be any good) without. Amanda is a brilliant director, producer, and writer, and her skill at all of these things is matched only by her unflinching commitment to lifting other women up. Whether it is mentoring, passing along a résumé, or donating her time, funds, or manual labor (she built the bookshelf in my house), Amanda is a true feminist fighter—and an amazing friend.

To the team of editors and advisors who helped make this book a reality, in particular my agent Howard Yoon (along with Gail Ross) at RossYoon and my editor Julie Will at HarperWave. Howard encouraged this idea from the very beginning, when it was just a blip of a column, and Julie was absolutely unflinching in her enthusiasm from its early days. Between the two of them, you could fill a 64G iPhone with the frantic messages sent at all hours by this author; yet they handled it with grace, humor, and patience. Thank you.

Thank you to Sarah Ball, whose brilliant behind-the-scenes wordsmithing I owe credit to many, if not all, my favorite lines, and who helped me out of many a narrative jam; to Susanna Schrobsdorff, my longtime editor at *Time* and the ultimate "boast bitch," who has never *not* touched a piece of writing I have been most proud of; to Rachel Simmons, my partner-in-trendspotting, whose friendship, bathroom humor, and always even-keeled wisdom have helped guide me through this process. Thank you to Lizzy Bailey Wolf, a doctoral student at Harvard Business School, who helped ensure that every last claim in this book was backed up by research, and that that research was not being misstated; to the absolute pro Amy Ryan, whom I would happily share a copyediting pen with any day; and last but not least, to my wonderful illustrators Saskia Wariner and Hilary Fitzgerald Campbell, as well as Harper designer Leah Carlson-Stanisic, who expertly helped inject visual humor and brought my words to life on the page.

Much like the ethos of this book, its writing truly would not have happened without the vast support of an extended fight club who offered up endless wisdom, read early drafts, endured two a.m. freakouts, sat for interviews, starred in a video, and whose general badassery inspires me daily. There are too many to name, but a special thanks to:

Sheryl Sandberg, who taught me to back every assertion up with data, who somehow manages to be as good with words as she is with business, who found time to give feedback on every last sentence of this book, and whose resilience inspires me daily.

Casey Schwartz, my constant advisor, mental-health-BFF-support-team of one, and a truly brilliant editor and friend.

My research crew, who helped with every piece of this book but also made writing it *fun*: Sharon Attia, Jordana Narin, Jing Qu (honorary), and Evan Zavidow. I am so proud of each of you—you are the future!!!!

To Lucia Aniello, Ashley Bearden, Hillary Buckholtz, Cristen Conger, Nell Constantinople, Jena Friedman, Ilana Glazer, Jill Goodwin, Halle Kiefer, Swanna MacNair, Asie Mohtarez, Kate Mullaney, Shauna Pinkett, Smita Reddy, Danielle Klang Thomson, Sarah Shepard, Nell Scovell, and Stephanie Smith: you women make me want to raise a fist and perfect my eyebrow arc all at the same time.

The women of the List, and in particular founders Rachel Sklar and Glynnis MacNicol, who have made a business out of helping women; Ruby Sklar, second-tiniest member of the fight club; the whip smart Tanya Tarr, who—without ever having met me—read every last chapter and offered notes; digital strategy whiz Kate Gardiner; event planning maestro Katie Longmyer; and so many others whose wisdom and advice have seeped into the pages of this book.

Putting out a book is a bit like launching a small startup, and I could not have done it without the friends, and sometimes strangers, who chipped in, from design to event planning to every last e-mail introduction it apparently takes to get a book off the ground:

To Rich Tong and the team at FohrCard, including Penelope Tong, Grace Murray, and Emma Hetherington, who launched my website, stayed up late into the night helping me review layouts, and helped strategize all aspects of my marketing plan, usually over whiskey.

To my partner in vision quests and personal branding COO Sara

Wilson, who setup meetings, pitched me for speeches, and cheerily sat through dozens of conference calls on my behalf.

To the extended team at HarperWave, including Karen Rinaldi, Brian Perrin, Rachel Elinsky, and Kate Lyons.

To the design guru Monica Parra; the comedian Andy Haynes; master negotiator Emanuel Neuman; PBOD chair Susie Banikarim; Makers rockstars Dyllan McGee, Sammi Leibovitz, and Blair Enders; the always-quotable Libby Leffler; video extraordinaire Luisa Guerrero; actors-in-their-spare-time Brittany Gooden, Ebonee Williams, Nick Scott, Kai Mathews, PJ Evans, Sanjay Ginde, Barrett Sheridan, Noah Shannon, Joe Lazauskus, Morgan Fletcher, Aixsha Hiciano, Alex Shoushtari, and Jaye Bartell; zine queen Allison Maloney; LA besties Rachel Webber, Frankie Shaw, Micah Fitzerman-Blue, and Liba Rubenstein (and Zelda!); Aminatou Sow of *Call Your Girlfriend*; Yng-Ru Chen at Tattly; Shanna Nash at SNASH Jewelry (check out her feminist rings!); Joanna Coles and Sara Austin at *Cosmopolitan*; Gina Gotthilf at Duolingo; PR whizzes Alisa Richter and Laura Barganier; honorary roomie Giulia Heimen; Brooklyn besties Matt and Patty Slutsky; lactation advisors Rosie Bancroft, Abby Slonecker, Anna Gall, and Lyndsi Rashkow; the great Jenn Needleman; Gia Milinovich, a stranger on the Internet who gifted me feministfightclub.com out of pure feminist camaraderie.

To the incredible team at Lean In, who supported this endeavor from the beginning and have inspired me (and it) in so many ways: Nola Barackman, Gina Bianchini, Marianne Cooper, Elizabeth Diana, Ashley Finch, Charlton Gholson, Debi Hemmeter, Hannah Kay Herdlinger, Kelly Hoffman, Anne Kornblut, Tessa Lyons, Katie Miserany, Mana Nakagawa, Kelly Parisi, Jeanne Ready, Raena Saddler,

Andrea Saul, Elliot Schrage, Nicole Stiffle, Rachel Thomas, Ashley Zandy, and the ever-wise (and witty) David Dreyer and Eric London. Leaning the f–k in every damn day.

To the experts and academics who took the time to read chapters, allowed me to observe them, shared their research, and helped walk me through it: the wonderful Adam Grant at Wharton Business School, who—in addition to doing a TED Talk, writing a bestselling book, and teaching, among other things—offered absolutely invaluable feedback; the linguists Robin Lakoff and Deborah Tannen, whose work on gender and language I have long admired, and to whom I owe the chapter on speech; to Sally Roesch Wagner, a feminist fighter since before I knew the definition of the word, who reminded me that feminism can be *fun*; thank you to Barbara Berg, Hannah Riley Bowles, Joan C. Williams, Gretchen McCulloch, and Bill Hoogterp, whom I will always think of when I say "like" and "um."

To Jeff Roth at *New York Times* morgue, to whom I have to thank for the fascinating historical tidbits you'll find throughout these pages and with whom I would gladly spend hours on end locked in a sub-basement surrounded by news clippings. To my editors at the *Times*, Laura Marmor and Stuart Emmerich, thank you for being all-around-awesome and continuing to publish my columns even as I became increasingly frazzled by the book.

To the *Newsweek* Dollies, who inspired this all in the very first place, and in particular Lucy Howard, Pat Lynden, Lynn Povich, Marc Peyser, and my forever-partners-in-byline (and friendship) Jesse Ellison and the aforementioned Ms. Ball. This book would not exist without you.

To my parents, Veronica Mratinich and Jim Benvenga, who raised

ACKNOWLEDGMENTS

us to be feminists; who somehow instilled in my brothers and I that if something was unjust we should speak out in protest of it. Not everybody has that privilege, and I have recognized over the years that my power lies in words on the page. To my brothers Nick and Zach Benvenga, the members of my *first*-ever fight club, thank you for toughening me up early.

And finally, to the main men in my life, Sam Slaughter and Charles the Dog Brownlips, who endured many late nights and early mornings, brought snacks when I couldn't remember how many days it had been since I'd slept or showered, who dutifully supported me throughout this process, and peed on my research only once (Charles not Sam). You are the best duo a feminist could come home to.

NOTES

INTRODUCTION

xxvi male peers do: American Association of University Women, "Graduating to a Pay Gap," 2012, http://www.aauw.org/files/2013/02/graduating-to-a-pay-gap-the-earnings-of-women-and-men-one-year-after-college-graduation.pdf.

xxvi negotiate a raise: Linda Babcock and Sarah Laschever, *Women Don't Ask,* http://www.womendontask.com/stats.html.

xxvi more collaborative: Facebook gender bias training, https://managingbias.fb.com.

xxvi more profitable: Cristian L. Dezsö and David Gaddis Ross, "Does Female Representation in Top Management Improve Firm Performance? A Panel Data Investigation," *Strategic Management Journal* 33, no. 9 (September 2012): 1072–89; Cedric Herring, "Does Diversity Pay? Race, Gender, and the Business Case for Diversity," *American Sociological Review* 74, no. 2 (April 2009): 208–24.

xxvi More inclusive: Alison Cook and Christy Glass, "Do Women Advance Equity? The Effect of Gender Leadership Composition on LGBT-Friendly Policies in American Firms," *Human Relations,* forthcoming, 2016.

xxvi more effective leaders: Samantha C. Paustian-Underdahl, Lisa Slattery Walker, and David J. Woehr, "Gender and Perceptions of Leadership Effectiveness: A Meta-Analysis of Contextual Moderators," *Journal of Applied Psychology* 99, no. 6 (January 2013): 1129–45.

xxvi take unnecessary risks: Brad M. Barber and Terrance Odean, "Boys Will Be Boys: Gender, Overconfidence, and Common Stock Investment," *The Quarterly Journal of Economics* 116, no. 1 (February 2001): 261–92.

xxvi great at multitasking: Katty Kay and Claire Shipman, *The Confidence Code: The Science and Art of Self-Assurance—What Women Should Know* (New York: Harper Collins, 2014), 113.

xxvi higher emotional intelligence: Dana L. Joseph and Daniel A. Newman, "Emotional Intelligence: An Integrative Meta-Analysis and Cascading Model," *Journal of Applied Psychology* 95, no. 1 (January 2010): 54–78, http://psycnet.apa.org/index.cfm?fa=buy.optionToBuy&id=2010-00343-013.

xxvi by 26 percent: McKinsey Global Institute, *How Advancing Women's Equality Can Add $12 Trillion to Global Growth,* 2015, http://www.mckinsey.com/global-themes/employment-and-growth/how-advancing-womens-equality-can-add-12-trillion-to-global-growth.

xxvi (and they do): Steven H. Appelbaum, Lynda Audet, and Joanne C. Miller, "Gender and Leadership? Leadership and Gender? A Journey through the Landscape of Theories," *Leadership and Organization Development Journal,* 24, no. 1 (2003): 43–51.

PART 1

7 women in professional meetings: Christopher F. Karpowitz, Tali Mendelberg, and Lee Shaker, "Gender Inequality in Deliberative Participation," *American Political Science Review* (August 2012): 1–15, http://www.bu.edu/wgs/files/2014/12/Karpowitz-et-al.-2012.pdf.

7 they interrupt more frequently: Marianne LaFrance, "Gender and Interruptions: Individual Infraction or Violation of the Social Order?" *Psychology of Women Quarterly* 16 (1992): 497–512, http://interruptions.net/literature/LaFrance-PWQ92.pdf; Kristin J. Anderson and Campbell Leaper, "Meta-Analyses of Gender Effects on Conversational Interruption: Who, What, When, Where, and How," *Sex Roles* 39, nos. 3–4 (1998): 225–52, http://www.ffri.hr/~ibrdar/komunikacija/seminari/Anderson,%20 1998%20-%20Meta-alnalyses%20of%20gender%20effects%20on%20convers.doc.

7 twice as likely: Adrienne Hancock and Benjamin Rubin, "Influence of Communication Partner's Gender on Language," *Journal of Language and Social Psychology,* May 11, 2014, http://jls.sagepub.com/content/early/2014/05/09/0261927X14533197; Victoria L. Brescoll, "Who Takes the Floor and Why: Gender, Power, and Volubility in Organizations," *Administrative Science Quarterly* 56, no. 4 (December 2011): 622–41.

9 less likely to be interrupted: Carol W. Kennedy and Carl Camden, "Interruptions and Nonverbal Gender Differences," *Journal of Nonverbal Behavior* 8, no. 2 (December 1983): 91–108.9 get a good seat: Kathryn Heath, Jill Flynn, and Mary Davis Holt, "Women, Find Your Voice," *Harvard Business Review,* June 2014, https://hbr.org/2014/06/women-find-your-voice.

11 still ending up with credit: Heather Sarsons, "Gender Differences in Recognition for Group Work," Working Paper, December 3, 2015, http://scholar.harvard.edu/sarsons/publications/note-gender-differences-recognition-group-work.

11 correctly attributed to them: Facebook gender bias training; Madeline E. Heilman and Michelle C. Haynes, "No Credit Where Credit Is Due: Attributional Rationalization of Women's Success in Male-Female Teams," *Journal of Applied Psychology* 90, no. 5 (September 2005): 905–16, http://dx.doi.org/10.1037/0021-9010.90.5.905.

17   fall to women: Sheryl Sandberg and Adam Grant, "Madam C.E.O., Get Me a Coffee," *New York Times,* February 6, 2015, http://www.nytimes.com/2015/02/08/opinion/sunday/sheryl-sandberg-and-adam-grant-on-women-doing-office-housework.html.

19   mansplained to Abigail: Lyman Abbott, "Why Women Do Not Wish the Suffrage," *The Atlantic,* September 1903, http://www.theatlantic.com/past/docs/issues/03sep/0309suffrage.htm.

23   more influence when they do: Sandberg and Grant, "Madam C.E.O., Get Me a Coffee."

25   why women shouldn't become astronauts: National Public Radio, "What Happens When You Get Your Period in Space?" September 17, 2015, http://www.npr.org/sections/health-shots/2015/09/17/441160250/what-happens-when-you-get-your-period-in-space.

26   emphasize why they're upset: Brescoll and Uhlmann, "Can an Angry Woman Get Ahead?"; Joan C. Williams and Rachel Dempsey, *What Works for Women at Work: Four Patterns Working Women Need to Know* (New York: NYU Press, 2014), 100.

29   with similar qualifications: Shelley J. Correll, Stephen Benard, and In Paik, "Is There a Motherhood Penalty?," *American Journal of Sociology* 112, no. 5 (March 2007): 1297–339, http://gender.stanford.edu/sites/default/files/motherhoodpenalty.pdf; Joan C. Williams, coauthor, *What Works for Women at Work: Four Patterns Working Women Need to Know,* in a video produced for LeanIn.Org, http://leanin.org/education/what-works-for-women-at-work-part-3-maternal-wall/;based on calculations by Correll, Benard, and in Paik; "Is There a Motherhood Penalty?," *American Journal of Sociology,* 2007, http://gender.stanford.edu/sites/default/files/motherhoodpenalty.pdf.

29   breadwinners in their homes: Williams and Dempsey, *What Works for Women at Work.*

30   than those without: LeanIn.Org and McKinsey & Co., *Women in the Workplace 2015,* http://womenintheworkplace.com/ui/pdfs/Women_in_the_Workplace_2015.pdf.

30   a single sentence: Beatriz Aranda and Peter Glick, "Signaling Devotion to Work over Family Undermines the Motherhood Penalty," *Group Processes and Intergroup Relations,* May 23, 2013, http://gpi.sagepub.com/content/early/2013/05/22/1368430213485996.abstract.

31   more productive: Boris B. Baltes et al., Flexible and Compressed Workweek Schedules: A Meta-Analysis of Their Effects on Work-Related Criteria, *Journal of Applied Psychology,* 1999, https://www.researchgate.net/publication/232480680_Flexible_and_Compressed_Workweek_Schedules_A_Meta-Analysis_of_Their_Effects_on_Work-Related_Criteria.

43   *competence* from *confidence*: Tomas Chamorro-Premuzic, "Why Do So Many Incompetent Men Become Leaders?," *Harvard Business Review,* August 22, 2013, https://hbr.org/2013/08/why-do-so-many-incompetent-men.

43   men perceive their work as better: Sheryl Sandberg, *Lean In* (New York: Knopf, 2013).

46   athletics helps *breed* female leaders: EY Women Athletes Business Network and espnW, *Making the Connection: Women, Sport and Leadership*, 2014, http://www. ey.com/GL/en/Newsroom/News-releases/news-female-executives-say-participation-in-sport-helps-accelerate–leadership-and-career-potential.

PART 2

55   credit for it: Sheryl Sandberg and Adam Grant, "Madam C.E.O., Get Me a Coffee," *New York Times,* February 6, 2015, http://www.nytimes.com/2015/02/08/opinion/sunday/sheryl-sandberg-and-adam-grant-on-women-doing-office-housework.html.

55   for black and Latina women: Joan C. Williams, Katherine Phillips, and Erika Hall, *Double Jeopardy? Gender Bias Against Women of Color in Science,* WorkLifeLaw, UC Hastings College of Law, 2015, http://www.uchastings.edu/news/articles/2015/01/williams-double-jeopardy-report.php.

55   raises, and bonuses: Madeline E. Heilman and Julie J. Chen, "Same Behavior, Different Consequences: Reactions to Men's and Women's Altruistic Citizenship Behavior," *Journal of Applied Psychology* 90, no. 3 (May 2005): 431–41, http://psycnet. apa.org/journals/apl/90/3/431/.

57   behind the scenes: Sandberg and Grant, "Madam C.E.O., Get Me a Coffee."

59   "help from others," or "luck": Sylvia Beyer, "Gender Differences in Causal Attributions by College Students of Performance on Course Examinations," *Current Psychology* 17, no. 4 (1998): 346–58.

59   "modest" in the process: Jessi L. Smith and Meghan Huntoon, "Women's Bragging Rights: Overcoming Modesty Norms to Facilitate Women's Self-Promotion," *Psychology of Women Quarterly,* December 20, 2013, http://intl-pwq.sagepub.com/content/early/2013/12/20/0361684313515840.abstract.

60   give away more credit: Michelle Haynes and Madeline Heilman, "It Had to Be You (Not Me)! Women's Attributional Rationalization of Their Contribution to Successful Joint Work Outcomes," *Personality and Social Psychology Bulletin,* May 7, 2013, http://psp.sagepub.com/content/early/2013/05/03/0146167213486358.full, http://www.eurekalert.org/pub_releases/2013–05/sfpa-wws050713.php.

60   for the team's work: Heather Sarsons, "Gender Differences in Recognition for Group Work," Working Paper, December 3, 2015, http://scholar.harvard.edu/files/sarsons/files/gender_groupwork.pdf?m=1449178759; Haynes and Heilman, "It Had to Be You (Not Me)!"

63   when women decline they are penalized: Heilman and Chen, "Same Behavior, Different Consequences"; Lise Vesterlund, Linda Babcock, and Laurie Weingart, "Breaking the Glass Ceiling with 'No': Gender Differences in Declining Requests for Non Promotable Tasks," Carnegie Mellon Working Paper, 2013, http://gap.hks.

harvard.edu/breaking-glass-ceiling-%E2%80%9Cno%E2%80%9D-gender-
differences-declining-requests-non%E2%80%90promotable-tasks.

64   out of obligation: Ellen Langer and Arthur Blank, "The Mindlessness of Ostensibly Thoughtful Action: The Role of 'Placebic' Information in Interpersonal Interaction," *Journal of Personality and Social Psychology* 36, no. 6 (1978): 635–42.

65   guilty about it: Katharine Ridgway O'Brien, "Just Saying 'No': An Examination
of Gender Differences in the Ability to Decline Requests in the Workplace," Society
for Industrial and Organizational Psychology, 2015. http://scholarship.rice.edu/
bitstream/handle/1911/77421/OBRIEN DOCUMENT_2014.pdf.

65   women say yes more frequently than men: Ibid.

65   underestimating how likely: Ibid.

67   93 percent: Albert Mehrabian, *Silent Messages: Implicit Communication of Emotions and Attitudes* (Belmont, California: Wadsworth Publishing Company, 1981).

68   in job interviews: Unpublished interview with author, 2014; Amy J. C. Cuddy,
Caroline A. Wilmuth, Andy J. Yap, and Dana R. Carney, "Preparatory Power Posing
Affects Nonverbal Presence and Job Interview Performance," *Journal of Applied Psy-
chology*, February 9, 2015, http://dx.doi.org/10.1037/a0038543.

69   women occupy less space: Baden Eunson, *Communicating in the 21st Century*, chapter 7, http://www.johnwiley.com.au/highered/eunson2e/content018/web_
chapters/eunson2e_web7.pdf.

69   as more confident: Judith A. Hall, Erik J. Coats, and Lavonia Smith LeBeau, "Non-
verbal Behavior and the Vertical Dimension of Social Relations: A Meta-Analysis,"
Psychological Bulletin 131, no. 6 (2005): 898–924, http://www.wisebrain.org/papers/
NonverbCommVerticalRels.pdf.

71   increase your confidence: Dana R. Carney, Amy J. C. Cuddy, and Andy J. Yap,
"Power Posing: Brief Nonverbal Displays Affect Neuroendocrine Levels and Risk Tol-
erance," *Psychological Science* 21, no. 10 (October 2010): 1363–68.

72   notebook in hand: "When the Career Woman Vies with Man," *New York Times
Magazine*, October 26, 1930.

75   less they speak: Christopher F. Karpowitz, Tali Mendelberg, and Lee Shaker,
"Gender Inequality in Deliberative Participation," *American Political Science Review*
(August 2012): 1–15, http://www.bu.edu/wgs/files/2014/12/Karpowitz-et-al.-2012.pdf.

75   in mixed-sex groups: Melissa C. Thomas-Hunt and Katherine W. Phillips, "When
What You Know Is Not Enough: Expertise and Gender Dynamics in Task Groups,"
Personal Social Psychology Bulletin 30, no. 12 (December 2004): 1585–98, http://psp.
sagepub.com/content/30/12/1585.abstract.

76   and shout commands: Deborah Tannen, *Talking 9 to 5: Women and Men at Work*
(New York: William Morrow, 1983), http://academic.luzerne.edu/shousenick/101–
COMPARE-CONTRAST_article_Tannen.doc.

76   formal (and prepared): Kathryn Heath, Jill Flynn, and Mary Davis Holt, "Women,

Find Your Voice," *Harvard Business Review,* June 2014, https://hbr.org/2014/06/women-find-your-voice.

77   (and garner support): Ibid.

79   cocky or immodest: Olivia A. O'Neill and Charles A. O'Reilly III, "Reducing the Backlash Effect: Self-Monitoring and Women's Promotions," *Journal of Occupational and Organizational Psychology,* 2011, http://www.alphagalileo.org/AssetViewer.aspx?AssetId=40772&CultureCode=en.

80   insincerity looks worse: Ovul Sezer, Francesca Gino, and Michael I. Norton. "Humble-Bragging: A Distinct—and Ineffective—Self-Presentation Strategy," Harvard Business School Working Paper, no. 15-080, April 2015.

80   who bragged openly: Michael D. Robinson, Joel T. Johnson, and Stephanie A. Shields, "On the Advantages of Modesty: The Benefits of a Balanced Self-Presentation," *Communication Research* 22, no. 5 (October 1995): 575–91, http://crx.sagepub.com/content/22/5/575.abstract.

81   Again: science: Vera Hoorens, Mario Pandelaere, Frans Oldersma, and Constantine Sedikides, "The Hubris Hypothesis: You Can Self-Enhance, But You'd Better Not Show It," *Journal of Personality* 80, no. 5 (October 2012): 1237–74, http://onlinelibrary.wiley.com/doi/10.1111/j.1467–6494.2011.00759.x/abstract.

81   boast on your behalf: Jeffrey Pfeffer, Christina T. Fong, Robert B. Cialdini, and Rebecca R. Portnoy, "Overcoming the Self-Promotion Dilemma: Interpersonal Attraction and Extra Help as a Consequence of Who Sings One's Praises," *Personal Social Psychology Bulletin,* October 2006, http://psp.sagepub.com/content/32/10/1362.short.

83   leave than men: Ashley Milne-Tyte, "Women Stay in Jobs Longer Than They Should," *Marketplace,* July 17, 2013, http://www.marketplace.org/2013/07/17/economy/women-stay-jobs-longer-they-should.

85   negative performance reviews: Venessa Wong, "Women Prefer Male Bosses Even More Than Men Do," *Bloomberg,* October 16, 2014, http://www.bloomberg.com/news/articles/2014-10-16/women-dislike-having-female-bosses-more-than-men-do.

85   95 percent of working women: Peggy Drexler, "Are Queen Bees Real?" *Forbes,* October 17, 2014, http://www.forbes.com/sites/peggydrexler/2014/10/17/are-queen-bees-real/#1391e85c83a1.

87   conflict among women perceived differently: Leah D. Sheppard and Karl Aquino, "Much Ado About Nothing? Observers' Problematization of Women's Same-Sex Conflict at Work," *Academy of Management Perspectives* 27, no. 1, (2013): 52–62.

87   senior women feel: Joan C. Williams and Rachel Dempsey, *What Works for Women at Work: Four Patterns Working Women Need to Know* (New York: NYU Press, 2014), 264; Robin J. Ely, "The Effects of Organizational Demographics and Social Identity on Relationships Among Professional Women," *Administrative Science Quarterly* 39, no. 2 (June 1994): 203–38, http://www.jstor.org/stable/2393234?seq=1#page_scan_tab_contents.

90   common among high-achieving: Valerie Young, *The Secret Thoughts of Success-ful Women: Why Capable People Suffer from Imposter Syndrome and How to Thrive in Spite of It* (New York, Crown Business: 2011).

92   nerve-wracking event: Laura Starecheski, "Why Saying Is Believing—The Science of Self-Talk," National Public Radio, October 30, 2014, http://www.npr.org/sections/health-shots/2014/10/07/353292408/why-saying-is-believing-the-science-of-self-talk.

93   "fooled by somebody else": Claire Shipman and Katty Kay, *The Confidence Code: The Science and Art of Self-Assurance—What Women Should Know* (New York: Harper-Collins, 2014).

96   any "visible effort": Sara Rimer, "Social Expectations Pressuring Women at Duke, Study Finds," *New York Times*, September 24, 2003.

96   she's a woman of color: Ashleigh Shelby Rosette and Robert W. Livingston, "Fail-ure is not an option for Black women: Effects of organizational performance on leaders with single versus dual-subordinate identities," *Journal of Experimental Social Psy-chology* 48 (2012) 1162–11167; V. L. Brescoll, E. Dawson, & E. L. Uhlmann. "Hard won and easily lost: The fragile status of leaders in gender-stereotype-incongruent occupa-tions." *Psychological Science,* 2010; Joan C Williams and Rachel Dempsey, *What Works for Women at Work: Four Patterns Women Need to Know* (New York: NYU Press, 2014), 228.

97   gateway to success: Angela L. Duckworth et al., "Grit: Perseverance and Passion for Long-Term Goals," *Journal of Personality and Social Psychology*, 2007, https://www.sas.upenn.edu/~duckwort/images/Grit%20JPSP.pdf.

97   huge amount of stress: Carsten Wrosch, Michael F. Scheier, Gregory E. Miller, Richard Schulz, and Charles S. Carver, "Adaptive Self-Regulation of Unattainable Goals: Goal Disengagement, Goal Reengagement, and Subjective Well-Being," *Person-ality and Social Psychology Bulletin*, 2003; Carston Wrosch et al., "The Importance of Goal Disengagement in Adaptive Self-Regulation: When Giving Up is Beneficial," *Self and Identity*, 2: 1–20, 2003, https://www.researchgate.net/profile/Carsten_Wrosch/publication/233264292_The_Importance_of_Goal_Disengagement_in_Adap-tive_Self-Regulation_When_Giving_Up_is_Benef   icial/links/0c960533315d-f7b28c000000.pdf. Society for Personality and Social Psychology, 2003, https://www.researchgate.net/profile/Carsten_Wrosch/publication/233264292_The_Importance_of_Goal_Disengagement_in_Adaptive_Self-Regulation_When_Giving_Up_is_Beneficial/links/0c960533315df7b28c000000.pdf.

100   Gender differences in burnout: A meta-analysis, by Radostina K. Purvanova, John P. Muros, *Journal of Vocational Behavior*, 77, no. 2, (October 2010): 168–85. http://www.sciencedirect.com/science/article/pii/S0001879110000771.

100   worn out most days: Radostina K. Purvanova and John P. Muros, "Gender Differ-ences in Burnout: A Meta-Analysis," *Journal of Vocational Behavior* 77, no. 2 (October 2010): 168–85, http://www.sciencedirect.com/science/article/pii/S0001879110000771; Centers for Disease Control and Prevention, Percentage of Adults Who Often Felt Very Tired or Exhausted in the Past 3 Months, by Sex and Age Group, National Health

Interview Survey, United States, 2010–2011, http://www.cdc.gov/mmwr/preview/mmwrhtml/mm6214a5.htm.

100   negatively affects women's health: Youngjoo Cha, "Overwork and the Persistence of Gender Segregation in Occupations," *Gender & Society* 27 (April 2013): 158–84, http://gas.sagepub.com/content/27/2/158.full?keytype=ref&siteid=spgas&ijkey=an5gkkROnpdx2; Youngjoo Cha, "Overwork, Underwork, and the Health of Men and Women in the United States," March 29, 2013, unpublished paper, http://paa2013.princeton.edu/papers/132394.

100   on women's shoulders: U.S. Bureau of Labor Statistics, American Time Use Survey Summary, June 24, 2015, http://www.bls.gov/news.release/atus.nr0.htm; "Overwork and the Persistence of Gender Segregation in Occupations," *Gender & Society* 27 (April 2013): 158–84, http://gas.sagepub.com/content/27/2/158.full?keytype=ref&siteid=spgas&ijkey=an5gkkROnpdx2.

102   according to Pew: Pew Research Center, "Another Gender Gap: Men Spend More Time in Leisure Activities," June 10, 2013, http://www.pewresearch.org/fact-tank/2013/06/10/another-gender-gap-men-spend-more-time-in-leisure-activities.

103   twice as hard, right: Catriona Harvey-Jenner, "Women Need More Sleep Than Men and That's a FACT," *Cosmopolitan,* March 4, 2016.

PART 3

110   hold their female managers to different standards: Sharon Mavin, "Queen Bees, Wannabees and Afraid to Bees: No More Best Enemies for Women in Management?," *British Journal of Management* 19, no. s1 (March 2008): S75–84, http://papers.ssrn.com/sol3/papers.cfm?abstract_id=1095907.

110   prefer male to female bosses: Gallup, "Americans Still Prefer a Male Boss to a Female Boss," October 2014, http://www.gallup.com/poll/178484/americans-prefer-male-boss-female-boss.aspx.

113   her professional status: Marianne Cooper, "For Women Leaders, Likability and Success Hardly Go Hand-in-Hand," *Harvard Business Review,* April 30, 2013, https://hbr.org/2013/04/for-women-leaders-likability-a/.

113   hard to swallow: Madeline E. Heilman et al., "Penalties for Success: Reactions to Women Who Succeed at Male Gender-Typed Tasks," *Journal of Applied Psychology,* 2004, http://search.committee.module.rutgers.edu/pdf/Heilman%20adn%20Wallen%202004.pdf; Laurie A. Rudman and Peter Glick, "Prescriptive Gender Stereotypes and Backlash Toward Agentic Women," *Journal of Social Issues,* 2001, http://web.natur.cuni.cz/~houdek3/papers/Rudman%20Glick%202001.pdf; Kathleen L. McGinn and Nicole Tempest, "Heidi Roizen," Harvard Business School Case 800-228, January 2000, revised April 2010, http://hbr.org/product/Heidi-Roizen/an/800228-PDF-ENG.

114   in male terms: Interview with author, 2010.

115   deficient in the other: Amy Cuddy, "Just Because I'm Nice, Don't Assume I'm Dumb," *Harvard Business Review,* February 2009.

116   skill level at all: Paula Szuchman, "Are Recommendation Letters Biased Against Women?," *Wall Street Journal,* November 15, 2010, http://blogs.wsj.com/juggle /2010/11/15/are-recommendation-letters-biased-against-women/.

116   as being pushovers: Ibid.

121   chillier working conditions: Lynn Peril, *Swimming in the Steno Pool: A Retro Guide to Making It in the Office* (New York: W.W. Norton, 2011), 203.

122   "as a national policy": The Center for Legislative Archives online, http://congress archives.tumblr.com/post/37712637089/on-december-11-1917-alice-wadsworth-president.

125   "passionate": Stephanie A. Shields, "Passionate Men, Emotional Women: Psychology Constructs Gender Difference in the Late 19th Century, *History of Psychology* 10, no. 2, (2007): 92–110.

126   Remember that group: Veronica Rocha and Lee Romney, "Black Women Kicked off Napa Wine Train to Sue for Discrimination," *Los Angeles Times,* October 1, 2015.

126   to one group: Roxanne A. Donovan, "Tough or Tender: (Dis)Similarities in White College Students' Perceptions of Black and White Women," *Psychology of Women Quarterly* 35 (3): 2011458–68, *Psychology of Woemn Quarterly* 35 (3) 2011: 458–68.

126   "Angry Black Woman": Alessandra Stanley, "Wrought in Rhimes's Image," *New York Times,* September 18, 2014.

126   "Am I being the Angry Black Woman?": Huda Hassan, "The Angry Black Woman Must Die," BuzzFeed, July 31, 2015.

132   report feeling stalled: LeanIn.Org and McKinsey & Co., *Women in the Workplace 2015,* http://womenintheworkplace.com/ui/pdfs/Women_in_the_Workplace_2015.pdf; Sylvia Ann Hewlett and Tai Green, "Black Women Ready to Lead," Center for Talent Innovation, 2015, http://www.talentinnovation.org/_private/assets/Black WomenReadyToLead_ExecSumm-CTI.pdf.

132   a white-sounding name: Marianne Bertrand and Sendhil Mullainathan, "Are Emily and Greg More Employable than Lakisha and Jamal? A Field Experiment on Labor Market Discrimination." The National Bureau of Economic Research, 2003, http://www.nber.org/papers/w9873.

134   village of male Smurfs: Jay Newton-Small, *Broad Influence: How Women Are Changing the Way America Works* (New York: TIME, 2015).

134   behalf of *all* women: Rosabeth Moss Kanter, "Some Effects of Proportions on Group Life: Skewed Sex Ratios and Responses to Token Women," *American Journal of Sociology,* 82, no. 5 (March 1977): 965–90.

136   with junior women: Kimberly E. O'Brien et al., "A Meta-Analytic Investigation of Gender Differences in Mentoring," *Journal of Management,* 35, no. 2, (2010): 537–54; Herminia Ibarra, Nancy M. Carter, and Christine Silva, "Why Men Still Get More Promotions than Women," *Harvard Business Review,* September 2010; Sylvia Ann Hewlett et al., "The Sponsor Effect: Breaking Through the Last Glass Ceiling," *Harvard*

Business Review Research Report, December 2010, 35; Kim Elsesser, *Sex and the Office: Women, Men, and the Sex Partition That's Dividing the Workplace* (New York: Taylor Trade Publishing, 2015). (The first statistic comes from research by the economist Sylvia Ann Hewlett).

139   Verge of a catfight: Leah D. Sheppard and Karl Aquino, "Much Ado About Nothing? Observers' Problematization of Women's Same-Sex Conflict at Work," *Academy of Management Perspectives* 27, no. 1 (2013): 52–62.

139   done by women: Madeline E. Heilman, "Description and Prescription: How Gender Stereotypes Prevent Women's Ascent up the Organizational Ladder," *Journal of Social Issues*, 57, no. 4, (Winter 2001): 657–74.

140   noticed more and remembered longer: Joan C. Williams and Rachel Dempsey, *What Works for Women at Work: Four Patterns Working Women Need to Know* (New York: NYU Press, 2014), 228; C. M. Steele, S. J. Spencer, & J. Aronson, (2002). "Contending with group image: The psychology of stereotype and social identity threat," http://disjointedthinking.jeffhughes.ca/wp-content/uploads/2011/07/Steele-Spencer-Aronson-2002.-Contending-with-group-image.pdf.

140   you don't belong: Andy Martens, Michael Johns, Jeff Greenberg, and Jeff Schimel, "Combating stereotype threat: The effect of self-affirmation on women's intellectual performance." *Journal of Experimental Social Psychology* 42, (2006): 236–43; Marguerite Rigoglioso, "Simple Interventions Bridge the Achievement Gap Between Latino and White Students," *Stanford University News*, February 14, 2013, http://news.stanford.edu/news/2013/february/latino-achievement-gap-021413.html.

142   perform more confidently: Ioana M. Latu, Marianne Schmid Mast, Joris Lammers, and Dario Bombari, "Successful Female Leaders Empower Women's Behavior in Leadership Tasks," *Journal of Experimental Social Psychology* 49, no. 3 (May 2013): 444–48.

143   tap out at thirty: Chris Wilson, "This Chart Shows Hollywood's Glaring Gender Gap," *Time*, October 6, 2015.

143   candidate was female: Jessica Bennett, "The Beauty Advantage," *Newsweek*, July 19, 2010.

146   white male peers: Alison Cook and Christy Glass, "Above the Glass Ceiling: When Are Women and Racial/Ethnic Minorities Promoted to CEO?," *Strategic Management Journal* 35, no. 7 (July 2014): 1080–89; Ken Favaro, Per-Ola Karlsson, and Gary L. Neilson, "Women CEOs of the last 10 years," PwC Strategy&, April 29, 2014, http://www.strategyand.pwc.com/reports/2013-chief-executive-study.

147   because we're female: Michelle K. Ryan, S. Alexander Haslam, Mette D. Hersby, and Renata Bongiorno, "Think Crisis–Think Female: The Glass Cliff and Contextual Variation in the Think Manager–Think Male Stereotype," *Journal of Applied Psychology* 96, no. 3 (2011): 470–84, https://www.uni-klu.ac.at/gender/downloads/FP_Ryan_2011.pdf.

149   could barely speak: Tom Lutz, *Crying: The Natural and Cultural History of Tears,* chapter 1, https://www.nytimes.com/books/first/l/lutz-crying.html; Sandra Newman, "Man, Weeping," *Aeon,* September 9, 2015.

150   ancient proverb proclaimed: Lutz, *Crying.*

150   a tear or two: Ibid.

150   with a colleague: Unpublished research by Kimberly Elsbach of the University of California, Davis; Olga Khazan, "Lean In to Crying at Work," *The Atlantic,* March 17, 2016.

151   crying more *visible*: Anne Kreamer, "Why Do Women Cry More Than Men?," *The Daily Beast,* December 18, 2010, http://www.thedailybeast.com/articles/2010/12/18/john-boehner-crying-why-do-women-cry-more-than-men.html; Richard H. Post, "Tear Duct Size Differences of Age, Sex and Race," Department of Human Genetics, University of Michigan Medical School, https://deepblue.lib.umich.edu/bitstream/handle/2027.42/37483/1330300109_ftp.pdf?sequence=1.

152   "It's happening everywhere": Jessica Bennett, "Why So Many Women Are Crying at the Gym," *Time,* October 20, 2014.

153   you'll likely be crying at the feet of a man: "Why the Dearth of Statues Honoring Women in Statuary Hall and Elsewhere?," *Washington Post,* April 17, 2011.

PART 4

159   even less trustworthy: Jin Ko Sei, C. M. Judd, and D. A. Stapel, "Stereotyping Based on Voice in the Presence of Individuating Information: Vocal Femininity Affects Perceived Competence but Not Warmth," *Personal Social Psychology Bulletin* 35, no. 2 (February 2009): 198–211; R. C. Anderson, C. A. Klofstad, W. J. Mayew, and M. Venkatachalam, "Vocal Fry May Undermine the Success of Young Women in the Labor Market," *PLoS One* 9, no. 5 (2014), http://www.ncbi.nlm.nih.gov/pmc/articles/PMC4037169/.

165   true for men: Jan Hoffman, "Overturning the Myth of Valley Girl Speak," *New York Times,* December 23, 2013; Caroline Winter, "What Does How You Talk Have to Do with How You Get Ahead?" *Bloomberg,* April 24, 2014.

167   cutting you off: Amanda Ritchar and Amalia Arvanito, "The Form and Use of Uptalk in Southern Californian English," presentation made at the 166th ASA Meeting in San Francisco, December 5, 2013, http://acoustics.org/pressroom/httpdocs/166th/4pSCa2-Ritchart.html.

169   "authority and control": Ellen Petry Leanse, "Just Say No," *LinkedIn Pulse,* May 29, 2015.

172   among young women: Rich Smith, "I Feel Like We Say 'I Feel Like' All the Time," *The Stranger,* July 15, 2015.

172   groups, shouting commands: Deborah Tannen, interview with author.

172   oh-so-many feels: Joan C. Williams and Rachel Dempsey, *What Works for Women at Work: Four Patterns Working Women Need to Know* (New York: NYU Press, 2014), 66.

172   "for clear thought": Phyllis Mindell, Ed.D., *How to Say It for Women* (New York: Prentice Hall Press, 2001).

173   way to communicate: Deanna Geddes and Lisa T. Stickney, "Muted Anger in the Workplace: Changing the 'Sound' of Employee Emotion Through Social Sharing," 2012, http://papers.ssrn.com/sol3/papers.cfm?abstract_id=2731708.

175   more than women: Douglas Quenqua, "They're, Like, Way Ahead of the Linguistic Currrrve," *New York Times,* February 27, 2012, http://www.nytimes.com/2012/02/28/science/young-women-often-trendsetters-in-vocal-patterns.html.

176   to a listener: Ann Friedman, "Can We Just, Like, Get Over the Way Women Talk?" *New York,* July 9, 2015.

178   women who suffer: Anderson et al., "Vocal Fry May Undermine the Success of Young Women in the Labor Market."

179   a Stanford linguist: "What's the Big Deal About Vocal Fry? An NYU Linguist Weighs In," *NYU News,* September 29, 2015, https://www.nyu.edu/about/news-publications/nyu-stories/lisa-davidson-on-vocal-fry.html.

179   a 2014 study: Anderson, "Vocal Fry May Undermine the Success of Young Women."

181   largely used by women: Jessica Bennett and Rachel Simmons, "Kisses and Hugs in the Office," *The Atlantic,* December 2012.

185   actually build trust: Roderick I. Swaab et al., "Early Words That Work: When and How Virtual Linguistic Mimicry Facilitates Negotiation Outcomes," *Journal of Experimental Social Psychology* 47, no. 3 (May 2011): 616–21.

188   politicians at all: Women's Media Center, "Name It. Change It. Findings from an Online Dial Survey of 800 Likely Voters Nationwide," 2010, http://www.lakeresearch.com/news/NameItChangeIt/NameItChangeIt.pres.pdf.

189   "size 6": R.W., "Obituary: Geraldine Ferraro," *Economist,* May 27, 2011, http://www.economist.com/blogs/democracyinamerica/2011/03/obituary.

192   female teaching assistant: Bellack, Marisa, "I Was Gay Talese's Teaching Assistant. I Quit Because of His Sexism," *Washington Post,* April 9, 2016, https://www.washingtonpost.com/posteverything/wp/2016/04/09/gay-talese-sexism/.

PART 5

197   OK to do: "Women Negotiate Better for Themselves If They're Told It's OK to Do So," *Harvard Business Review,* September 2014, https://hbr.org/2014/09/women-negotiate-better-for-themselves-if-theyre-told-its-ok-to-do-so/; Deborah A. Small, Michele Gelfand, Linda Babcock, and Hilary Gettman, "Who Goes to the Bargaining Table? The Influence of Gender and Framing on the Initiation of Negotiation," *Journal of Personality and Social Psychology* 93, no. 4 (2007): 600–13.

199 Hispanics make fifty-four: American Association of University Women, "The Simple Truth about the Gender Pay Gap," Spring 2016, http://www.aauw.org/research/the-simple-truth-about-the-gender-pay-gap/.

199 male peers do: American Association of University Women, "Graduating to a Pay Gap: The Earnings of Women and Men One Year after College Graduation," 2013, http://www.aauw.org/files/2013/03/Graduating-to-a-Pay-Gap-The-Earnings-of-Women-and-Men-One-Year-after-College-Graduation-Executive-Summary-and-Recommendations.pdf.

200 when they do: Jessica Bennett, "How to Attack the Gender Wage Gap? Speak Up," *New York Times,* December 15, 2012.

200 those who don't: Fiona Greig, "Propensity to Negotiate and Career Advancement: Evidence from an Investment Bank That Women Are on a 'Slow Elevator,'" *Negotiation Journal* 24 no. 4 (October 2008): 495–508.

200 get the job: Linda Babcock and Sara Laschever, *Women Don't Ask: Negotiation and the Gender Divide* (Princeton, NJ: Princeton University Press, 2003) http://www.womendontask.com/stats.html.

200 both women and men: Nolan Feeney, "Study: Women More Likely to Be Lied to in Negotiations Than Men," *Time,* August 3, 2014; Laura J. Kray, Jessica A. Kennedy, and Alex B. Van Zant, Not competent enough to know the difference? Gender stereotypes about women's ease of being misled predict negotiator deception, Organizational Behavior and Human Decision Processes, November 2014.

204 50 cents more in the final agreement: Chris Guthrie and Dan Orr, "Anchoring, Information, Expertise, and Negotiation: New Insights from Meta-Analysis," *Ohio State Journal on Dispute Resolution,* 2006.

206 seen as 'pushy': Hannah Riley Bowles and Linda Babcock, "How Can Women Escape the Compensation Negotiation Dilemma? Relational Accounts Are One Answer," *Psychology of Women Quarterly* 37, no. 1 (2013): 80–96.

206 "bring to the job": Hannah Riley Bowles, "Why Women Don't Negotiate Their Job Offers," *Harvard Business Review,* June 19, 2014, https://hbr.org/2014/06/why-women-dont-negotiate-their-job-offers/.

207 Ask for advice: Bowles and Babcock, "How Can Women Escape the Compensation Negotiation Dilemma?"

207 unless they smile: Hannah Riley Bowles, Linda Babcock, and Lei Lai, "Social incentives for gender differences in the propensity to initiate negotiations: Sometimes it does hurt to ask," *Organizational Behavior and Human Decision Processes,* 103 (1), (2007): 84–103.

208 to compromise quickly: Jennifer L. Holt and Cynthia James DeVore, "Culture, Gender, Organizational Role, and Styles of Conflict Resolution: A Meta-Analysis," *International Journal of Intercultural Relations* 29 (2005): 165–96.

PART 6

220   she was sure: Carla A. Harris, *Expect to Win: 10 Proven Strategies for Thriving in the Workplace* (New York: Plume Books, 2010).

220   just *60 percent*: Georges Desvaux, Sandrine Devillard-Hoellinger, and Mary C. Meaney, "A Business Case for Women," *The McKinsey Quarterly,* September 2008, 4, http://www.womenscolleges.org/files/pdfs/BusinessCaseforWomen.pdf.

220   theirs as worse: Katty Kay and Claire Shipman, *The Confidence Code: The Science and Art of Self-Assurance—What Women Should Know* (New York: HarperCollins, 2014), 19; "Yet Another Explanation for Why Fewer Women Make it to the Top," *Washington Post,* April 1, 2011, https://www.washingtonpost.com/blogs/post-leadership/post/yet-another-explanation-for-why-fewer-women-make-it-to-the-top/2011/04/01/gIQA2IIP9N_blog.html.

222   deliver their return: Claire Martin, "Wearing Your Failures on Your Sleeve," *New York Times,* November 8, 2014.

222   believe its personal: Sheryl Sandberg, *Lean In* (New York: Knopf, 2013).

222   women's fear of failure: "Gender Study Shows Women Are 'Driven by Fear of Failure,'" *Times Higher Education,* November 6, 1998, https://www.timeshighereducation.com/news/gender-study-shows-women-are-driven-by-fear-of-failure/109745.article.

222   already good at: James P. Byrnes, David C. Miller, and William D. Schafer, "Gender Differences in Risk Taking: A Meta-Analysis," *Psychological Bulletin* 125, no. 3 (May 1999): 367–83; Catherine C. Eckel and Phillip J. Grossman, "Men, Women, and Risk Aversion: Experimental Evidence," in *Handbook of Experimental Economics Results,* vol. 1, ed. Charles R. Plott and Vernon L. Smith (Amsterdam: North Holland, 2008), 1061–73.

223   two kinds of failures: Adam Grant, *Originals: How Non-Conformists Move the World* (New York: Viking Books, 2016).

223   not the failure itself: Thomas Gilovich and Victoria Husted Medvec, "The Experience of Regret: What, When, and Why," *Psychological Review* 102, no. 2 (April 1995): 379–95, http://dx.doi.org/10.1037/0033-295X.102.2.379.

224   harder time saying no: Madeline E. Heilman and Julie J. Chen, "Same behavior, different consequences: Reactions to men's and women's altruistic citizenship behavior," *Journal of Applied Psychology* 90, (2005): 431–41; Lise Vesterlund, Linda Babcock, Laurie Weingart, "Breaking the Glass Ceiling with 'No': Gender Differences in Declining Requests for Non-Promotable Tasks," 2013, http://gap.hks.harvard.edu/breaking-glass-ceiling-%E2%80%9Cno%E2%80%9D-gender-differences-declining-requests-non%E2%80%90promotable-tasks; Katharine Ridgway O'Brien, "Just Saying 'No': An Examination of Gender Differences in the Ability to Decline Requests in the Workplace," thesis, Rice University, 2014, https://scholarship.rice.edu/handle/1911/77421?show=full.

226   at Boston University: Neil Irwin, "How Some Men Fake an 80-Hour Workweek, and Why It Matters," *New York Times,* May 4, 2015; Original research: Erin Reid, "Embracing, Passing, Revealing, and the Ideal Worker Image: How People Navigate Expected and Experienced Professional Identities," *Organizational Science,* April 20, 2015.

227   women shy away from risk: Catherine C. Eckel and Phillip J. Grossman, "Men, Women, and Risk Aversion: Experimental Evidence," in C. Plott and V. Smith, ed. *Handbook of Experimental Economics Results,* vol 1. Ch. 113, 1061–73, 2008; Doug Sundheim, "Do Women Take as Many Risks as Men?," *Harvard Business Review,* February 27, 2013, https://hbr.org/2013/02/do-women-take-as-many-risks-as/.

229   to a much greater degree: Ibid.

240   correctly attributed to them: Facebook gender bias training, https://managing-bias.fb.com; No Credit Where Credit Is Due: Attributional Rationalization of Women's Success in Male-Female Teams. Madeline E. Heilman; Michelle C. Haynes, *Journal of Applied Psychology,* Vol 90 (5): Sep 2005, 905–916. http://dx.doi.org/10.1037/0021-9010.90.5.905.

240   generous team player: Eugene Caruso, Nicholas Epley, and Max H. Bazerman, "The Costs and Benefits of Undoing Egocentric Responsibility Assessments in Groups," *Journal of Personality and Social Psychology* 91, no. 5 (November 2006): 857–71.

240   fifteen-degree angle more: Baden Eunson, *Communicating in the 21st Century,* chapter 7, http://www.johnwiley.com.au/highered/eunson2e/content018/web_chapters/eunson2e_web7.pdf.

241   talk more than we do: Christopher F. Karpowitz, Tali Mendelberg, and Lee Shaker, "Gender Inequality in Deliberative Participation," *American Political Science Review* (August 2012): 1–15, http://www.bu.edu/wgs/files/2014/12/Karpowitz-et-al.-2012.pdf.

242   falls to women: Sheryl Sandberg and Adam Grant, "Madam C.E.O., Get Me a Coffee," *New York Times,* February, 2015, http://www.nytimes.com/2015/02/08/opinion/Sunday/sheryl-sandberg-and-adam-grant-on-women-doing-office-housework.html.

242   you guys benefit: Joan C. Williams and Rachel Dempsey, *What Works for Women at Work: Four Patterns Working Women Need to Know* (New York: NYU Press, 2014); Madeline E. Heilman and Julie J. Chen, "Same Behavior, Different Consequences: Reactions to Men's and Women's Altruistic Citizenship Behavior," *Journal of Applied Psychology* 90 no. 3 (May 2005) 431–41, http://dx.doi.org/10.1037/0021-9010.90.3.431.

243   more sex with their wives: Constance Gager and Scott Yabiku, "Who Has the Time? The Relationship Between Household Labor Time and Sexual Frequency," *Journal of Family Issues,* February 2010.

243   burnt out, resentful: Scott Coltrane, "Research on Household Labor: Modeling and Measuring the Social Embeddedness of Routine Family Work," *Journal of Marriage and Family,* November 2000.

243   split chores, decisions and finances more evenly: Lourdes Garcia-Navarro, "Same-Sex Couples May Have More Egalitarian Relationships," NPR's *All Things Considered*, December 29, 2014.

243   good for all kids: B. Heilman, G. Cole, K. Matos, A. Hassink, R. Mincy, G. Barker, "State of America's Fathers: A MenCare Advocacy Publication," Washington, DC: Promundo-US. *http://men-care.org/soaf/download/PRO16001_Americas_Father_web. pdf*.

243   limit their career aspirations: A. Croft, T. Scmader, K. Block, A. S. Baron, "The Second Shift Reflected in the Second Generation: Do Parents' Gender Roles at Home Predict Children's Aspirations?," *Psychological Science*, July 2014.

244   happier in their jobs: Jamie Ladge, Beth Humberd, Brad Harrington, and Marla Watkins, "Updating the Organization Man: An Examination of Involved Fathering in the Workplace," *Academy of Management Perspectives*, October 7, 2014.

244   live longer: Stephanie L. Brown, Dylan M. Smith, Richard Schulz, Mohammed U. Kabeto, Peter A. Ubel, Michael Poulin, Jaehee Yi, Catherine Kim, and Kenneth M. Langa, "Caregiving Behavior Is Associated with Decreased Mortality Risk," *Psychological Science*, April 2009.

244   more collaborative: Facebook unconscious bias training, https://managingbias. fb.com.

244   more profitable: Cristian L. Dezsö and David Gaddis Ross, "Does Female Representation in Top Management Improve Firm Performance? A Panel Data Investigation," *Strategic Management Journal* 33, no. 9 (September 2012): 1072–89; Cedric Herring, "Does Diversity Pay? Race, Gender, and the Business Case for Diversity," *American Sociological Review* 74, no. 2 (April 2009): 208–24.

244   More inclusive: Alison Cook and Christy Glass, (2016). "Do women advance equity? The effect of gender leadership composition on LGBT-friendly policies in American firms." *Human Relations* (forthcoming).

JOIN THE FEMINIST FIGHT CLUB!

254   with her husband: Marilyn Yalom and Theresa Donovan Brow, *The Social Sex: A History of Female Friendship* (New York: Harper Perennial, 2015).

ABOUT THE AUTHOR

Jessica Bennett is an award-winning journalist and critic who writes on women, sexuality, and culture. She is a columnist at the *New York Times*, where you can regularly find her byline in the Sunday style section on topics ranging from feminist sororities to female pot entrepreneurs to the psychological hell of that little text bubble that pops up on your iPhone when somebody is typing (or not typing). She recently authored the first profile of Monica Lewinsky in a decade, capturing her plight to redefine her story. Jessica is also a contributing editor at LeanIn.org, the nonprofit founded by Sheryl Sandberg, where she cofounded and curates the Lean In Collection, a photo partnership with Getty Images to change the way women are depicted in stock photography.

He just wanted a decent book to read ...

Not too much to ask, is it? It was in 1935 when Allen Lane, Managing Director of Bodley Head Publishers, stood on a platform at Exeter railway station looking for something good to read on his journey back to London. His choice was limited to popular magazines and poor-quality paperbacks – the same choice faced every day by the vast majority of readers, few of whom could afford hardbacks. Lane's disappointment and subsequent anger at the range of books generally available led him to found a company – and change the world.

'We believed in the existence in this country of a vast reading public for intelligent books at a low price, and staked everything on it'
Sir Allen Lane, 1902–1970, founder of Penguin Books

The quality paperback had arrived – and not just in bookshops. Lane was adamant that his Penguins should appear in chain stores and tobacconists, and should cost no more than a packet of cigarettes.

Reading habits (and cigarette prices) have changed since 1935, but Penguin still believes in publishing the best books for everybody to enjoy. We still believe that good design costs no more than bad design, and we still believe that quality books published passionately and responsibly make the world a better place.

So wherever you see the little bird – whether it's on a piece of prize-winning literary fiction or a celebrity autobiography, political tour de force or historical masterpiece, a serial-killer thriller, reference book, world classic or a piece of pure escapism – you can bet that it represents the very best that the genre has to offer.

Whatever you like to read – trust Penguin.